The Energy Revolution

It's Free. It's Clean.
It's Everywhere

By
Jeremy W. Gorman

Copyright © 2016 by Jeremy Gorman
All rights reserved.
Green Ivy Publishing
1 Lincoln Centre
18W140 Butterfield Road
Suite 1500
Oakbrook Terrace IL 60181-4843
www.greenivybooks.com

ISBN: 978-1-945379-03-1

Preface

Everyone needs energy. That's what gets things done. We keep increasing our demand for energy because we want to do more. So energy has become the largest industry in the world—except for food. Today, 80% of our energy comes from fossil fuels—what I call **Old Energy**. That puts **Big Energy** (fossil fuel suppliers and utilities) in control of both domestic and commercial energy. If you want electricity, you get it from Big Energy. If you want heat for your home, Big Energy is where you get it. If you want to go somewhere, Big Energy supplies the fuel. They are entrenched—BUT!

There is more **New Energy** (sun, wind, hydroelectric, tidal, and geothermal) than Old Energy. It's everywhere! It's free! We have ignored it because Big Energy has made their fossil fuels the easiest source. They kept us uninformed on how to use New Energy. They keep us uninformed about the serious environmental damage that fossil fuels cause. That *keeps* them in control. Give them credit—they have made fossil fuels so easy to use that alternatives seemed too difficult to consider.

Old Energy pollutes our atmosphere and poisons our oceans. Unlike New Energy, it is finite, and we are using it up. Big Energy suppresses that information because they want to stay in control. *Your New Energy* shows you how to save money (and save the world) by forming **EnerJett** groups that bring free New Energy to entire neighborhoods. It shows you and your neighbors how Doing It Together (**DIT**), you can enjoy making your whole community energy independent.

Then you can have a neighborhood celebration and enjoy free energy permanently.

Standing the world's largest industry on its head is an enormous task. So it is also an enormous employment opportunity. Using New Energy will cut your energy bill, prevent further acidification of our oceans, and stop global warming. It will inhibit climate change and further increases in violent storms. Even more important, New Energy will employ thousands (millions?) of people locally. No long commutes to huge factories. Big Energy won't tell you how to do that. *Your New Energy* makes it fun! There is no excuse for having such a huge unemployment problem when so many New Energy challenges are crying for help.

Your New Energy has a different approach. We know we need to change our energy sources, but we think it is someone else's job. Instead of trying to get Big Energy to do what they believe will kill their market, this book wants to involve you in a massive cottage industry that uses local energy, local labor, and local materials. Government can't do it, and Big Energy won't. Let's not fight Big Energy. Make your own energy! Join the fun. Doing things is much better than sitting around munching on goodies while watching television. Avoid the obesity challenge.

With guidance from the website **Energettics.com**, you can meet new friends and learn fascinating new things. *Your New Energy* is your guide. Form an **EnerJett** group in your neighborhood. Follow the website Energettics.com, which explains clean New Energy. Put New Energy to use in all your neighborhood homes. Make it a game. Reward new ideas. Set goals and give prizes. Have completion parties. Challenge other **EnerJett** groups in adjoining neighborhoods. Do it together (**DIT**) and make new friends. Re-employ your local laid-off factory workers. They have the skills, and **Energettics.com** has the plan. Where else can you make new friends, learn fascinating new things, and save money? Life is about accomplishment. Here is a chance to accomplish something not just for you, but for all your neighbors as well. Got a better idea?

Your New Energy wants to start an energy revolution. It wants you in control of domestic energy—1/3 of Man's total energy demand. Because of Big Energy, few people know how to use New Energy. We keep asking Big Energy to make the change for us. But Old Energy is Big Energy's livelihood. They resist! *Your New Energy* makes New Energy fun, so you *want* to get involved. It explains solar energy and wind energy, and how you can get it free. It shows you and your neighbors how to use geothermal energy. The energy revolution is more than the change from Old Energy to New Energy. It is the change of *control* of domestic energy from Big Energy to *you*—the user! That is the energy revolution. Bye-bye, pollution! Farewell, climate change! So long, growing energy bills!

We have a worldwide unemployment problem today. Companies in industrial countries are building factories in depressed countries to capitalize on the low wages there. They are putting our skilled workers out of work. But there is no shortage of work to be done. Energy, the world's largest industry, is a major opportunity. Big Energy won't do that. Together, you can do it (DIT). Let Big Energy fend for itself. Countries like France and Spain are having serious unemployment problems and suffer depressed wages. Like Greece, they face bankruptcy. New

Energy is a huge opportunity for them. The energy we all need is everywhere. **EnerJett** groups can find and utilize it. That can create opportunity and local employment for millions of people.

Our continued, profligate abuse of fossil fuels could literally make this world uninhabitable in the next century. But don't become an **EnerJett** for fear! It is an opportunity to meet and work with your neighbors, to enjoy learning fascinating new technology, and to create a major increase in independence. How do you install solar panels or small rooftop wind generators? Why don't we use the energy of streams and rivers? Have rewards and completion parties. Make New Energy a positive social event. Remember—the thing that allowed Mankind to become the dominant species on earth was his ability to cooperate. What are you waiting for?

Contents

Preface		III
Introduction		1
Chapter 1	New Energy?	6
Chapter 2	Energettics	10
Chapter 3	DIT	15
Chapter 4	Conservation	20
Chapter 5	The Sun	25
Chapter 6	The Electric Conundrum	34
Chapter 7	Wind	41
Chapter 8	Geothermal Energy	50
Chapter 9	Tesla Free Energy	53
Chapter 10	New Hydro Energy	60
Chapter 11	Lunar Energy	65
Chapter 12	Batteries	68
Chapter 13	Recovering	71
Chapter 14	UrbanAg—Greening our Cities	76
Chapter 15	Ocean Currents	78
Chapter 16	DIT and Big Energy	80
Chapter 17	Wave energy	84
Chapter 18	Cost or investment?	86
Chapter 19	The Upside of Electronics	89
Chapter 20	Nuclear Energy—A Limited Resource	94

Introduction

Energy has become the largest industry in the world except for food—the source of your internal energy. But strangely, as we have increased our demand for energy, we have limited our sources of energy. Thousands of years ago, we used animal energy, firewood, wind, and water power—New Energy that arrived daily and allowed us to accomplish things we could not do ourselves. About 2,500 years ago, we discovered peat—Old Energy that was stored by nature in the fossils of once living things. Coal followed over 1,000 years ago, and because it was easy, soon dominated Man's energy supply. Set it on fire, and it could do things, like melting metals, that oxen and camels couldn't. For about 1,000 years, coal was our dominant source of energy. 160 years ago, we discovered oil, another fossil fuel. Because it was even easier than coal, it soon dominated our energy supply. Forget about horses and oxen. Forget about windmills and water wheels.

We overdid it! We became extremely wasteful of energy. Demand increased. Coal and oil became ever more difficult to obtain as we depleted these readily accessible natural resources. Prices increased. When I learned to drive, gasoline cost 18 cents per gallon. When my granddaughter learned to drive, it cost $4.50 per gallon. Today, we face a dilemma. If we keep increasing our demand for our dwindling Old Energy resources, we will use them up. And that's not the worst of it. By burning fossil fuels, we not only release million-year-old solar energy, we release million-year-old carbon into today's atmosphere as carbon dioxide.

It absorbs solar energy and warms our earth. It also acidifies our oceans. It is also raising our oceans as we melt our polar ice caps. We have skewed the delicate balance of nature that created and sustained all the life on today's Earth. Many species are showing severe stress. Mankind has caused the extinction of over three hundred species. If we continue, we could make Earth uninhabitable for many of today's living things—including Man!

Rejoice! New Energy abounds. Science has learned how to make use of it to get us off that destructive path. New Energy, like the people who use it, is everywhere. It cannot be used up and does not destroy the balance of nature. *Your New Energy* is your guidebook for learning and using New Energy. It shows you how to enjoy getting involved in saving money by saving Earth. We have allowed ourselves to become dependent upon Old Energy. But there is more New Energy than Old Energy. It arrives free every day. It is fascinatingly diverse, and we are still learning. How much sunlight does a solar panel convert into electricity? What is the best way to capitalize on wind energy? Can we build small water wheel generators in every stream in our convoluted world? Tides are on every shoreline in the world. Can't we use them?

Your New Energy takes a different approach to energy. Since everyone needs energy, everyone should be involved. But make involvement fun. Most of today's energy programs prompt Big Energy to introduce new science and new technology to the energy market. That further entrenches Big Energy. It gives them more control—and more profit. Why pay Big Energy to build giant windmills in the distant plains and ship electricity hundreds of miles to a user who has wind in his yard? *Your New Energy* wants to get *you* involved. It explains how to take control of domestic energy from corporate monopolies and put it in your hands. It shows you how to employ the skills of your unemployed neighborhood factory workers. Restoring the balance of nature will not only be rewarding, it will be fun. Look at the people you'll meet. Look at the things you'll learn. Look at the money you'll save. Look at the pride (and the party) you will have when you have made your neighborhood energy independent.

New Energy is enormous—but everyday people everywhere are even larger. This is a fascinating opportunity to learn and to be creative. If we Do It Together (**DIT**) it will be neither demanding nor burdensome. And look at the new friends you will make! Where else can you save money by saving Earth? Together, we can not only save Earth, we can meet new friends and save money. The whole idea of *Your New Energy* is to make domestic energy independence a game where we work together and have fun doing it. Got a better idea?

How do you get people to work together? You create a system of goals and rewards. It is human nature to enjoy accomplishment. You will need some money, so establish a small membership fee—$12-$25. I recommend establishing a dues program of a percentage (perhaps 10%) of the money members actually save after their savings have repaid their installation costs. New members' dues should be small ($2 or $3 per month) until their actions create actual energy savings. EnerJetts study local demands for energy. They look at the available New Energy sources in their neighborhood. Most of you feel you aren't getting what you need, or that you are paying too much. Find local sources of alternate energy on **Energettics.com** or on the Internet. Are you in a wind corridor? Do you have a stream in your neighborhood? Are you on a shoreline with tides? You are on land that is 55F° ten feet below the frost line everywhere. Geothermal systems tap into that vast energy reservoir.

Although the prime focus of **EnerJetts** is the individual home, there are many energy sources that apply to the whole neighborhood instead of just the individual home. If you are on a river or stream, the whole community would benefit from a small hydroelectric facility, or a series of small waterwheels. Geothermal heating can be used to help heat schools, apartments, or some commercial buildings.

EnerJett members pay for their own purchase and installation costs through their **EnerJett** group. This may take some capital investment that your treasury could help finance out of the dues you pay. It can provide low interest capital loans to its members for some of the more expensive projects like geothermal heating and cooling. And, of course, **EnerJetts** will arrange to pay those neighbors who install and maintain New Energy devices.

Start with conservation because it is the fastest and the cheapest way to save energy. **EnerJett** members should keep a record of the actual savings. Your group should establish a percentage of actual savings achieved as dues to pay for additional devices or programs that will save more money. Record keeping forms are available on **Energettics.com.** Establish goals for your **EnerJett** group, and have a party when they are achieved. Set the next goal at the party. One major goal for each member is the day they become energy independent. That's worth celebrating! You might connect with neighboring **EnerJett** groups and challenge them to a cost savings contest. Which can get the first energy independent member? Who can get the most energy independent homes? Which entire group can become energy independent first? Grounds for another party—and another goal!

Be sure that your group puts any new information it creates onto **Energettics.com**, so other **EnerJett** groups can learn from you as you have learned from them. **Energettics.com** should be continually growing as we all enjoy learning together.

Chapter 1

New Energy?

Since New Energy may well be the key to our continued existence on Earth, it is worth some clarification. What is New Energy? It is the energy that comes to us every day. It is overwhelmingly solar energy. But it is also wind energy, lunar energy, and geothermal energy from deep within the earth. It is not stored energy, like coal, gas, or oil. It is often called renewable energy, but that term can be misleading. Once used, energy is gone. It is not renewed—it is replaced. The sun does not restore yesterday's energy. It delivers New Energy to our earth 24/7. The term renewable energy was used to distinguish it from Old Energy—million-year-old solar energy that is stored in fossil fuels. That energy is not renewable either, but it does not come to us every day. Once used, it is gone.

Man is a prodigious consumer of energy. It was man's desire to accomplish things he could not do himself that sparked his all-consuming desire to find other sources of energy. Very early, we used animal power to help us do things we could not do ourselves—oxen, mules, camels, and horses pulled out stumps and hauled away boulders. We used wood fires to cook food and to allow us to move out of the tropics and stay warm. We kept searching for energy. Our technology was not yet developed, so early energy sources were primarily New Energy until we discovered peat about 2,500 years ago. That changed our focus to Old Energy because it was *easy*. So it soon dominated our energy sources. It was only about 200 years ago that we developed the science to use New Energy. We slowly began to develop the new technology that makes New Energy practical and competitive. That remains a long, but enjoyable, trip.

We also began to use outside energy to do things *instead* of doing it ourselves, like riding a horse or camel instead of walking or running. We sought as many sources of energy as we could, so energy became the world's largest industry (except for food). It is dominated by Old Energy, which Big Energy made easy. Unlike Old Energy, New Energy is everywhere, but our use of it has been impaired because Big Energy has made Old Energy *easier*. 80% of today's energy is Old Energy. That has consequences: Old Energy returns million-year-old carbon to today's atmosphere. We have increased the carbon content of the world's atmosphere 40% in one century and warmed our earth and oceans 2 degrees Fahrenheit by doing so. We are using up Old Energy. Oil and Gas reserves are seriously depleted and require drastic measures like "fracking" or arctic drilling to discover additional stored sources. We are extremely wasteful of energy, and, because the sources chosen are relatively inaccessible to the Man in the street, we become ever more dependent upon Big Energy for essentially all our energy needs.

No need! New Energy is everywhere. It comes in many elusive forms, like the sun, the wind, the heat within the earth, and the tides that are driven by the moon. More New Energy falls in your yard every day than you use. You ignore it because you have been convinced by Big Energy that their Old Energy is our best source of energy. But there is more New Energy than Old Energy, and, unlike Old Energy, you can't use it up. The New Energy that surrounds us is free once you learn how to capture it. That's what *Your New Energy* is all about. That is a significant factor in our overall energy picture. Old Energy has steadily increased not only its cost, but its portion of living expenses. More of your money goes to energy today than at any time in the past. New Energy can reverse that.

Give Big Energy credit. They have taken Old Energy that is scattered around Earth in inaccessible pockets and made it readily available to every human. You are not equipped to mine coal or drill for oil. Big Energy is! They have made their Old Energy *easy* to use. Not better—just *easy*. By doing so, Big Energy has come to dominate energy. They have control. You don't! If you want to heat or cool your house, you pay Big Energy. If you turn on your lights or run your dishwasher, you pay Big Energy. If you want to drive your car, you pay Big Energy. They are entrenched, and they love it. Major appliances are all designed to use Old Energy. New houses are not built without wires and some fuel resource.

There are problems with Old Energy that don't apply to New Energy. The use of fossil fuels takes million-year-old carbon and returns it to today's atmosphere as carbon dioxide. Burning coal also spews out toxic ingredients including mercury. Since carbon dioxide is an absorber of solar energy, we have warmed the earth, the atmosphere, and our oceans 2° Fahrenheit in one century. Carbon dioxide dissolves in water forming carbonic acid—the tangy ingredient in soda pop. Since 3/4 of our earth's surface is water exposed to air, the water dissolves the carbon dioxide and makes our lakes and oceans more acidic. We have increased the acidity (or to be more accurate, decreased the alkalinity) of our oceans by

9%. This is no small matter. Modern life had its origins in that water! Many marine species are having survival problems, and shellfish and corals are having trouble making their shells and structures. Man has already caused the extinction of over 300 species, and we are just beginning.

It may be hard to believe, but this massive world is in a delicate balance of climate and environment. As the seasons grow warmer, less ice is formed every winter and more ice melts every summer. So not only are our oceans getting more acidic, they are getting deeper. We have already increased the ocean level by eight inches, and at our current pace we will add another 4 or 6 feet this century. There go Florida's beaches! Chesapeake Bay, New York, and Boston harbors will have serious docking and shipping problems. Extreme predictions are a 20-foot rise—enough to flood London.

Warming our oceans 2°F has increased their evaporation—the largest energy transfer system on Earth—by 9%. We have tripled the number of violent storms. We are causing "climate change." Here is your opportunity to stop this assault.

Chapter 2

Energettics

Your New Energy offers opportunity. It is not a treatise of doom and gloom. New Energy does not pollute our atmosphere or our oceans with old carbon. It comes to us every day, so we cannot use it up. Since New Energy is everywhere, it need not be sent hundreds of miles to the user. There are dozens of books on the environment and on climate change, but few of them have solutions, and even fewer have solutions that involve you! A major theme of *Your New Energy* is the Do It Together (**DIT**) concept. Sharing this task will assure that it does not become a burden to **EnerJett** members. Cooperation is the major factor in man's dominance of this earth. Our ability to work together generated Mankind's success. Look around you. Every man-made thing you see is made by the cooperation of people. *Your New Energy* wants to help you work with each other toward worthy goals in energy--financial, environmental, and social reward. It presents a huge opportunity to make money by working with neighbors to save the environment and save the earth. A goal of *Your New Energy* is to create a massive cottage industry throughout the world. People can work together out of their own homes and neighborhoods on their own schedules—energy is everywhere, people are everywhere, and materials are everywhere. You don't need a massive factory to use local materials and labor to deliver local energy. The website **Energettics.com** and the Internet supply the know-how and the coordination. You and your **EnerJett** members supply the initiative. That can be fun!

An **EnerJett** chapter is a group of neighbors working together to make their neighborhood energy independent. **EnerJett** chapters have 5 to 50 members from their neighborhood. They meet weekly or monthly to identify the energy resources and the energy demands of their neighborhood. **EnerJett** chapters have access to **Energettics.com** where they find information on energy sources, equipment, assembly instructions, and safety requirements. It is their **DIT** coordinator.

Step one is to become an **EnerJett**. Join 3 or 4 of your neighbors and form a local chapter. You will need some money to get started, so a small ($10 to $50) membership fee may be needed. The idea is to *save* money, not *spend* it. Membership cards should be issued upon registration of your local **EnerJett** group. When you get 5 members, register and you will get a membership number and access to detailed instructions on **Energettics.com. Energettics.com** will have a forum where you can present your creative ideas for evaluation and development. We encourage interaction between chapters, which have different talents, different experience, and different needs. Remember, **Energettics** is a **DIT** enterprise. It will grow as its members learn and grow. If you find a new way to build solar panels, let us all know. If you have a new way to get geothermal energy, let us know. This is a challenging and exciting enterprise. We really want to make a better world to live in.

Your New Energy takes a different approach to energy. Instead of complaining about the massive Big Energy industry, work with them to create a world of free energy that grows *with* our environment instead of at the expense of it. Domestic energy is 1/3 of our expanding energy demand.

Rapid growth is pressing Big Energy to spend millions of dollars upgrading their 3-trillion-dollar obsolete hardware. They are upgrading high tension wires from 303,000 volts to 1,000,000 volts. They are "fracking" for natural gas. They drill for more oil in the Arctic waters. If you divert 1/3 of that rapid expansion, they will be able to invest that money in New Energy hardware instead of upgrading worn out and obsolete Old Energy hardware like the Keystone Pipeline to ship dirty oil sands 1,200 miles. **Energettics** will *increase* their profit margins because New Energy is free. They won't have to employ more coal miners and oil riggers. But don't fire them. Retrain them in New Energy. **EnerJett** jobs will be local and long term, unlike Keystone Pipeline jobs that will last a couple of years.

How many of you have worked with your close neighbors? The backyard fence meetings of 100 years ago are largely gone. Few neighborhoods enjoy each other like they did then. When I was in elementary school, I knew the names of every neighbor on our street. I knew their kids and played with them. Today, people working for big corporations tend to make their friends there instead of over the back fence. Here is an opportunity to create thousands of small groups with a focus on free, clean energy derived from local sources with local labor. Join your neighbors and form an **EnerJett** group. You will need a chairman, a secretary, and a treasurer. You may also need a construction manager. **EnerJetts** are informed and coordinated by the website **Energettics.com** as well as other Internet resources. They enjoy working together and learning together.

Your group should take a project-by-project approach. When you have found your optimum money-saving opportunity, one member should volunteer to be the first to try it. He will provide records of his recent energy expenses. The group may provide no interest loans to help him pay for the installation of the lowest cost/maximum return project in his home. The entire group will work together to install the chosen free-energy system and will all study the new energy cost and calculate the payback period. Here is where the opportunity for improvement arises. Could we do it better? Was this a better choice than another system? If the payback on the first system is under two years, everyone will want to have one. You are off and running!

You can all save half or more of your increasing energy bill. You can also put your ideas onto **Energettics.com** and help others worldwide. You can employ locally your unemployed or underemployed factory worker neighbors whose jobs were sent overseas. It is time to rediscover the cottage industry concept that built this country and many others as well. That is the essence of **DIT**. More than Do It Yourself (**DIY**), Do It Together (**DIT**) gets things done you can't do alone. Look at the fun you'll have. I suspect you may not know many local neighbors very well. I doubt that you do much with most of them. Here is your opportunity to find out how creative and enjoyable your neighbors are. You'll not only be surprised, you'll learn a lot and have a ball doing it.

Your New Energy is opportunity. Can you make solar panels produce more electricity or install them for less? Can you lower the cost and price of wind generators? If you are very clever, perhaps you can do both. Can you make a wind generator for under $300? Will it work 90% of the time on your roof or your neighbor's roof? Your goal is to make all your neighborhood homes energy independent. Save money, save the world, and gain control! *Your New Energy* has the answer to most of those problems and provides a path to the rest of the answers through **Energettics.com**. Together we can build a cooperative world for all of us.

Be sure to include social interaction. "All work and no play make Jack a dull boy." **EnerJetts** can play together just as they work together. Get the kids involved! If the project isn't fun, no one will volunteer. The job won't get done.

The technology to capitalize on New Energy is in its early stages of development. We are learning more every day. There is a wealth of information still to be uncovered, and finding it will be your great joy. When last did you have a neighborhood party? I'll bet the answer is never. Find out what you're missing. Did you know that one neighbor is a chef, and another knits fashionable sweaters? How come we have such a huge unemployment problem when there is so much fascinating work to be done right in your backyard with people you enjoy? Do you know how a solar panel works? Have you ever considered a windmill? Did you know that the earth under your foundation is 55°F even in winter? Life is about accomplishment. Don't let it get away!

Chapter 3

DIT

We have built a complex world and a culture where doing it yourself (**DIY**) often won't get the job done. Almost every structure you see around you was built by the co-operation of people working together. If we are going to stand the world's largest industry on its head, it will not be done by people working alone. We already have a massive energy industry upon which we are all dependent. We want to build and coordinate thousands of small groups that provide energy locally. **Energettics** is the ideal situation for such a concept because energy is everywhere, people are everywhere, and materials are everywhere. We don't need a huge factory to make windmills to be shipped hundreds of miles to people who could build and install them locally. A huge factory can't install solar panels on your roof. Your factory worker neighbor whose job was sent overseas would love to. A factory can't install a geothermal heating and hot water system in your home. With the guidance from **Energettics.com**, you and your neighbors can.

Behold the **EnerJett** group—a local group of people working together toward the goal of energy independence. Their goal is to make their community and every home in it energy independent with clean New Energy. Have you ever noticed that none of the many projects you have completed in your life got underway until you set a goal? The setting of the goal was the inspiration that started the action. Form an **EnerJett** chapter so that you and your neighbors can achieve the goal of energy independence. Then, set your first goal and *Do It Together* (**DIT**). The website **Energettics.com** is the guide that allows you to pool your diverse talents and become energy independent. It is more than a presentation of New Energy. It is a growing database of information on clean New Energy installation, safety requirements, and sources of tools and materials. It will include federal and state grants and loans. It has been devised as a forum for New Energy ideas and improvements. **EnerJetts** are the core of **Energettics.com**. They learn from it, they teach on it, they coordinate on it, they grow with it. Neighborhoods are ideal for this activity because neighbors come from a wide variety of backgrounds and have diverse talents. The New Energy industry is still new and has a lot of growing and learning to do. Get involved! You contribute to that advance when you become an **EnerJett**. Join or form a local **EnerJett** group and make your home and your neighborhood energy independent.

Energettics.com and your local **EnerJett** chapter are the fundamental operating units of **DIT**. Energy is a huge industry, and it will take lots of us to improve it. Working together is a critical part of this movement. You may not have all the skills for energy independence, but you and your neighbors do! No one has to move. No one has to sacrifice. Pool your skills and ideas to make an energy-independent world. The task is huge, and you can't do it alone. Standing the world's largest industry on its head will take lots of people, but there are seven billion of us. When we pool our resources, there is nothing we can't accomplish.

There is another reason for an **EnerJett** group. Not every New Energy source is fit for an individual home.

Tidal and hydro energy are almost everywhere but are not tiny sources that can be put into your home. They can and should be put in your neighborhood. **EnerJett** groups bring neighborhoods together so they can capitalize on all the New Energy sources available, not just those that can be put in or on your home. If your neighborhood is on a river or stream, your **EnerJetts** can install water wheels or build small dams that can capture that energy for your neighborhood. If you are on the shore line, you can capture tidal energy for your whole neighborhood.

Don't forget—people who work together can play together. Have contests and grand opening parties. Offer rewards for creative ideas. You might even want to go into competition with other nearby **EnerJett** groups to see which one can first achieve 50% or 75% or 100% of energy independence for their neighborhood. Man is a social animal, and your **EnerJett** group should contribute to that. Make it fun and inviting.

How do you form an **EnerJett** group? Bring a few neighbors together and register on **Energettics.com**. You will get a chapter number and some guidelines and membership cards. Pick a chapter name that characterizes your local neighborhood. Step one is to assess the local sources of New Energy that are available to your neighborhood. The New Energy industry has generated lots of used and broken equipment in its formative years, so seek and use the applicable equipment. (Try Ethos Energy.) Calculate the energy demand of the homes in your neighborhood. There will also be some recommendations for starting to get things done. You will need a little money to get underway. Charge a small membership fee—never more than

$50. You might consider a dues program, and I recommend that it is a small percentage of the participating member's actual savings (perhaps 10%) — small dues of $3 to $10 per month until devices are actually installed. That will inspire focused action on getting the job done. These funds will finance future projects as well as projects for the whole neighborhood in addition to the devices for individual homes. Each member pays for his own New Energy equipment and installation. Your **EnerJett** group can help members finance their first project. Provide him a record system (from **Energettics.com**) so he can see (and brag about) his actual savings. That will inspire reluctant neighbors to join your **EnerJett** group. It will also finance community (tidal or river) projects. The objective is to go stepwise toward energy independence starting with conservation and using those savings to finance further developments. Make it a game you can enjoy.

Every **EnerJett** meeting should have an objective and give small assignments to each member for reporting at the next meeting. Assignments can be about how to find used or damaged clean energy devices for minimal costs and upgrade to high performance. Groups should meet either monthly or perhaps weekly if several projects are underway. Meetings should be informative and focused. Keep them short — one hour max. Move them from home to home within the group. They should not be burdens, but enjoyable. Pick a chairman, a secretary, and a treasurer. Inject humor and warmth into your meetings. But remember that the bulk of the progress is not made in the meeting, but between meetings in the neighborhood.

You will need a website manager. That job can be fairly demanding, so it should be rotated among computer-wise members. They will get the group registered and get access to the resources on **Energettics.com**. More importantly, they will feed their learned information into **Energettics.com** so that it continues to grow and progress.

I would like to make an interesting point here. I am amazed at the number of TV ads I see that talk about retirement and how to enjoy it. I don't believe in retirement. Life is about accomplishment. Change of profession is the way to go. Pick some project you have wanted to do for years but didn't have the time to attack. Get going and get it done. Clean alternate energy is a particularly worthy project. Don't sit around, munching peanuts and watching TV. Get something done that you will be proud of. Don't join the obesity club of retired (and bored) people.

Chapter 4

Conservation

Most of us were brought up in a world of abundant energy. We learned wasteful habits. Simple things like leaving lights on when we leave a room or running hot water when we don't need it can consume substantial amounts of energy. Since most of us didn't even see the energy bills until we got our first home, we looked at energy as a part of our daily lives. Such attitudes persist in our lives and constitute 10% to 30% of our energy demand. The simple act of turning out the lights and turning down the heat or air conditioner in unoccupied rooms can reduce our energy bills noticeably. In extremely cold weather, you might turn the thermostat down 3 or 4 degrees and wear a sweater, jacket, or housecoat.

I have heard that keeping the temperatures at your lowest level of tolerance is beneficial to your health—your body becomes accustomed to the extra demand. Of course, putting on storm windows and caulking or sealing your windows can make large improvements in your energy efficiency. If you have an older home, putting more insulation under your roof or in your walls could make a big difference in your heating bill. Are your walls insulated? Probably not, if the building is more than forty years old or south of the Mason-Dixon line. That could be a major expense and very disruptive unless you can get the insulation blown in. The objective is to make improvements without handicapping you. Planning goes a long way toward that goal.

Did you know that it takes almost twice as much energy to cool a hot room as it does to heat a cold one? A fan blowing out the sunny-side window may do as much as running the air conditioner. Your habits are not evil practices, but ones learned in a different era, a time that failed to consider many of the side effects. The old coal furnaces, which few of us even remember, were frightfully inefficient. I remember as a child seeing black snow sometimes when I went out to go sledding. Our smoky coal furnaces coated everything black in the winter. When I was six, we moved to a gas heated house, and the black snow disappeared. I remember the unused, old coal furnace sitting beside the new gas furnace in our new basement.

The incandescent light bulb is inefficient—it converts about 3% of its electric energy into visible light. Fluorescent lights get about 10-12% of visible light from the electricity they consume. The new LEDs (Light Emitting Diodes) are even more efficient (15% to 22%). They are still new and expensive but have substantially longer life expectancy than either incandescent or fluorescent bulbs. If you have a creative bent, efficient lighting might be a challenge you would enjoy meeting. These problems are being solved, but many aren't quite ready for general consumption yet. Can you contribute?

A word of caution here! Fluorescent bulbs contain mercury. Mercury compounds are extremely toxic and must be avoided. There are special hazardous waste channels that should be carefully followed. We already have a serious mercury problem because coal also contains mercury, and we have been spewing coal smoke and ashes over this earth for a thousand years. We have seriously poisoned our oceans and are causing serious threats to some marine life. Since mercury compounds are so toxic, tiny amounts of them can cause extensive problems with many animals, particularly marine species; mercury tends to accumulate in marine habitats. Sea food is becoming a potential health threat as the mercury continues to accumulate. This is one factor that favors the use of LED lighting. That will change over time. Even today's high costs are economical if you consider their efficiency and their long life expectancy.

One energy waster is the clothes dryer. We have become enamored of the clothes dryer, which is an enormous consumer of energy. In about half of the laundry days of the year, we can do better hanging the clothes on a clothesline. People object to seeing their clothes flapping in the sterilizing sunlight, but it costs nothing and worked for hundreds of years. It actually reduces the need for ironing as well. If you live in an apartment, the flat roof could be a less visible clothes dryer. Putting up rooftop clotheslines and providing access could be a worthy **DIT** project for your **EnerJetts**. In the dead of winter, a clothes dryer may be required, but you could cut its usage by half with very little effort. If you have a basement, clotheslines can be installed there for winter use or on rainy days. You need not make a public display of your intimate wear.

Driving to work is a major energy consumer. Using smaller, fuel-efficient cars (mostly European models) makes a big difference. The American car is no longer primarily for transportation; it is a status symbol—the bigger, the more impressive. Carpooling helps. Finding neighbors who work close to where you work can cut energy consumption by 50% to 75%. Another **EnerJett** function? Combining shopping trips with neighbors will not only cut energy costs, it will become a pleasant get-together with neighbors. You can do your shopping or special appointments on your day in the rotation cycle. Many jobs today lend themselves to spending a day or two at home on the Internet rather than going to the office.

Don't forget public transportation. Most big cities have well-designed public transportation systems. In fact, your commute by public transportation will often be faster than driving your car. If you need to do shopping or make other appointments, pick one day per week to drive your car. Your car will last longer too. I favor bicycles since they also attack our national obesity problem. Kids should never be driven to school but walk or bicycle if they aren't on the school bus route. Cross-country skis in the winter? Roller-skates? Skateboards?

Riding lawnmowers and snow blowers encourage you to get fat and lazy. Is that what you want? If you have less than an acre of lawn, push your lawnmower for the exercise. Lack of exercise is a major health hazard today, but don't start a snow-shoveling program if you're over 65—it is the cause of many heart attacks in the elderly.

Many of us live in apartments with flat roofs. That area was once ground covered with vegetation that captured solar energy. Why not help clean our air by putting gardens and vegetation on those flat roofs? Inner-city kids might even make some money growing vegetables on the roof and selling them to their underfed neighbors. (See Chapter 14—**UrbanAg**.)

Your **EnerJett** group can find many creative ways to conserve energy. We need as many as possible on **Energettics.com**. Remember, this is a **DIT** project. Doing It Together puts more fun into projects. It is also a great education. But don't neglect another part of an **EnerJett** chapter—play together. When you achieve goals or finish projects, have a party. Celebrate—and set new goals.

Chapter 5

The Sun

By far our largest source of energy is the Sun. That is true of both Old Energy and New Energy. Old Energy is really solar energy stored in fossil fuels. Those fossils were once living matter, which drew their energy from the sun. Living things today still derive their energy from the sun. Our creator developed two kinds of living matter—plants (vegetation) and animals. Plants are basically sedentary absorbers of solar energy. They absorb primarily visible solar energy, which is only a portion of the sun's radiation. Vegetation is sedentary (the source of the term "to vegetate"). It doesn't move things around or accomplish things. Animals move all around and accomplish many things, but they can't absorb solar radiation—at least not enough to survive. So animals are dependent upon plants for survival. Meat eaters must recognize that the meat they eat was ultimately derived from vegetation. It would be wise for us to remember that as we cut down half of the world's forests and lay waste to acres of vegetation to make room for roads, homes, stores, factories, and apartment buildings.

Nothing lives forever. When living things die, they decay—a slow process that consumes much of the biological produce of life but retains that solar energy that supported them while alive. Carbon, the fundamental element to all living things, is the primary storage material for the energy of life. Fossil fuels (peat, coal, oil, and natural gas) are therefore the storage media for that old solar energy. Man has learned to burn that decayed material and recover the solar energy they store.

But the sun still shines today. That same energy that supported the dinosaurs still engulfs today's world as it did 40 million years ago. In the past 200 years, Man has learned how to capture and utilize much of that solar energy directly—New Energy. But the ease of getting energy from fossil fuels has stultified the development of those new solar sources. The science is far ahead of the technology to make use of it. There is more solar energy than all mankind uses. We use little now, but we will greatly expand its use in the future.

Big Energy is not a bad guy, although he has some bad guys in his fold. He is a very clever guy who made the use of fossil fuels so easy that we don't want to go anywhere else. But when he developed this Old Energy, he didn't plan for all the consequences thereof. He didn't know it would grow to such enormous proportions that we literally changed the world. When the light bulb was invented, there were 1.5 billion people on Earth. Only about 1/5 of them were able to use light bulbs, and less than 1% actually did. Today we have 7.5 billion people using artificial lighting. We didn't anticipate that we could consume all the massive fossil fuels with our profligate demand for energy. We didn't realize that we were literally changing the balance of nature that fostered all of today's living creatures.

We finally understood the evil of our ways about 60 years ago, but we were unprepared to make the necessary changes. Serious development of solar energy didn't even begin until about 50 years ago, but the development since then has been enormous. Prices for today's solar panels are about 15% of what their less-efficient predecessors were in 1970. We have learned much since, but we still have a long way to go, and most of today's world doesn't know how to make the necessary changes. The fossil fuel syndrome is entrenched. Every appliance you use was designed to make use of our fossil fuel-generated electricity. Big Energy loves it because it keeps them in control of energy with their fossil fuel sources.

Solar energy comes to us primarily (but not exclusively) by radiation—after all, we are 93 million miles from the sun. How else can that energy get here? There are many forms of radiation, which require different mechanisms to capture. The science is there, and it is a fertile field, but we face multiple problems. Much of the known science lacks the technology to make use of it. We don't yet have the equipment to utilize all the sun's bountiful energy—but we're learning. Most people don't, and probably aren't informed enough to make the changes. Big Energy has been so dominant in energy that they jealously guard their current advantages and oppose much of the needed changes while trying to entrench themselves further into our energy profile.

Energy decisions have been made almost exclusively for the profitability of Big Energy. (e.g. corn to ethanol—the Keystone Pipeline) Few people, including many in Big Energy, realize the risks we take by continuing that greedy approach to energy. These risks are indeed extremely serious, but they may not be quite as urgent as we often hear. To be honest, we don't know how urgent many of the environmental problems are, so waiting around for a disaster to tell us is foolish at best.

Because we all see it, visible solar radiation is our most developed source of solar energy. Even this needs some serious attention. Photovoltaic panels convert primarily visible solar radiation directly to electricity. Many materials convert sunlight into electricity in widely different efficiencies. Most are made from silicon. That is because 25% of the earth is silicon, so availability is the least of our problems. But silicon comes in several forms, which have differing abilities to absorb solar radiation. Because they are easy to make, most photovoltaic panels today are made from crystalline silicon. It isn't hard to make and can be reasonably economical. Of course, many manufacturers are more interested in making money than in saving the earth or their customer's money.

Crystalline silicon absorbs a range of solar radiation that does not match the sun's maximum output. Alloys of Silicon with some exotic elements often increase the amount of energy extractable from the sunshine. Amorphous silicon absorbs in a broader range of radiation wavelengths and can increase the output of a solar panel. Crystalline silicon panels convert about 22% of visible solar radiation to electricity. Amorphous silicon panels can convert from 25% to almost 30% of visible radiation. But amorphous panels are harder to make and are scarce and more expensive. There are even more expensive panels containing scarce atomic elements that can convert from 40% to almost 47% of visible solar radiation, which is only a maximum of 30% of total solar radiation. The rest of that radiation is converted to heat. That is why solar water heaters that convert all solar radiation to heat preceded photovoltaic systems by at least 50 years. That also causes many solar panels to overheat and lose efficiency. Perhaps this is an opportunity for your **EnerJett** group.

There are many solar panels on the market today. Most are assemblies of small solar cells about 2.5 inches by 5 inches each. There are quite a few variations of this, and many varieties are on the market. There is some standardization of these panels. 32 inch by 48 inch panels are quite common. They contain about 100 cells and produce from 12 to 24 volts of direct current (DC). Maximum output is generally 120 watts. Here is opportunity in spades. Your **EnerJett** group can learn how to install solar energy systems. Your **EnerJett** group may want to assemble solar panels from the solar cells that are on the market. Beware! Prices have enormous variation. (Cells from 10 cents per watt to over 75 cents are on eBay and other sources.) There also is a market for used or broken solar absorbers for your more creative **EnerJetts**. Instructions on making and installing solar panels are available on the Internet. "HomeMadeEnergy.org" markets DVDs and CDs on solar energy installation. There are courses in solar panel installation organized by the North American Board of Certified Energy Professionals (NABCEP). Kaplan University of Chicago, Illinois, has an extensive program of internet courses not only on solar panels installation, but on many other New Energy systems as well. Your local **EnerJetts** may want to enter one of their unemployed factory workers to one of those courses to become certified. Electric power installations usually require certified installers, as they should, because of the hazards of improper installation.

Solar absorption is not confined to photovoltaic panels. There are solar shingles. Many shingles are less efficient and convert only about 12% of solar radiation to useable energy, but that is changing rapidly and efficient shingles are already on the market. However, no shingles are as efficient as solar cells or panels. Shingles are less sensitive to the physical orientation of the roof but still need to face the sun. They are useless on north-facing roofs in the northern hemisphere and south-facing roofs in the southern hemisphere. They are much easier to install than solar panels, and because they are dual purpose (they have to seal the building against weather conditions), they may well become practical with a little further development. Because of their dual or even triple functions, they can be more cost effective than panels. They may become a major source of solar energy in the future.

Solar shingles may also have another potential. Today's photovoltaic panels ignore the infra-red radiation of the sun. In fact, many can overheat and lose their efficiency. There are panels designed specifically to generate heat from invisible infra-red solar radiation. In fact, they preceded photovoltaic panels on the market by about 50 years. They were used primarily to generate hot water, but were also used to help heat homes. The problem is that the demand is largest at night when there is no sun. Some solar shingles could have dual output—electricity from primarily visible light and heat from invisible infra-red radiation. Many are black or dark, so they can also absorb heat from infra-red radiation, which provides a reason for further development. I have seen none of these dual output shingles on the market. This is another **DIT** opportunity. How about stacking photovoltaic panels with clear backs on top of infrared panels to produce both heat and electricity from a single fixture? Can your **EnerJett** group do that? A few solar shingles already do.

Solar panels can be mounted in several ways. If the roof they occupy faces south (northern hemisphere) or quite close to south, they can be mounted directly on the roof. If not, they are usually mounted on racks that hold them facing the noon-day sun and at the optimum angle from horizontal to capture the largest practical amount of the local solar radiation. The sun rises and falls over our horizons, so adjusting the angle that makes the best use of the local solar radiation is important. Preferably the angle should be about 5 degrees more than the latitude. That will make them more productive earlier and later in the day when the sun is low in the sky. Some of us may want to install tracking devices that rotate the panels to keep them facing the sun continually. This complication requires some study to see if the performance supports the additional cost and the additional mounting and maintenance.

Currently, professionally installed solar panels feed their output into "inverters" that convert the output into higher voltage AC and feed it into the "Grid." The stated plan is that the utilities will pay you if you produce more than you use, but the real motive is to keep control of electricity in the hands of Big Energy. They are already lobbying to stop having to pay for extra electricity that you feed them. Besides, most of the new demand for electricity is for electronics that use the same low voltage DC that solar panels and shingles produce. But remember, a major advantage of New Energy is to have two sources of energy. When you feed your output into the grid, you eliminate that second source.

There is some concern about the use of metal for the mounting racks or stands. Note that they are usually the highest structure in the area and a prime target for lightning. They should preferably be made of wood or weatherproof plastic to avoid attracting lightning. There are also lightning rods.

There are also parabolic solar collectors designed to capture all the sun's radiation. These are primarily industrial units that focus that energy on pipes containing oil based liquids. They heat the fluids several hundred degrees and transfer the heat to a variety of commercial uses. These are primarily industrial installations and may not become much of a factor in domestic energy. Another **DIT** opportunity?

Don't quit yet. There are solar films that convert wide ranges of solar radiation to electricity. Some appear to produce both electricity and heat because they absorb a wide range of light wavelengths. This is still new technology—not so much new science—which has been around for a hundred years or so. There is a need for equipment to utilize that energy. *Your New Energy* sees this as a huge opportunity to develop the means to use New Energy and escape our dependence upon Old Energy. What are your ideas?

Many solar devices are available on the market today and can easily be found on the Internet. Most produce low voltage direct current (DC). You will not be able to feed that output into your vacuum cleaner or you washing machine. However, you can store DC in batteries and keep it available when the sun doesn't shine. There are numerous devices and systems on the open market for converting that DC into AC (inverters and alternators) for use in household appliances. But please note, the largest new electric demand is for electronics, which doesn't operate on commercial 115/230 volt AC. It uses the same low voltage DC that is created by photovoltaic systems. That's why you see a transformer on every electronic power line that converts commercial AC to electronic low voltage. Solar panels can eliminate thousands of those transformers.

It is probable that new construction will have two electric systems. New Energy tends to be low voltage and oriented toward electronic devices. Standard commercial electric systems are aimed primarily at appliances—washing machines, vacuum cleaners, clothes dryers and dishwashers. I suspect that more and more appliances in the future will use low voltage electricity like those for today's trailers and mobile homes. It is time we revised our electric usage to suit today's life style rather than that of 100 years ago. I would not cut down the power lines to your home yet.

It is worthy to note that AC is a more versatile form of electricity than DC. Wind turbines and water turbines can produce either AC or DC. Solar panels produce only DC. Your solar system should focus as much as possible on electronic uses because they closely match the voltage output of solar panels. Lighting is also seeing a strong movement toward low voltage. LED lighting is growing rapidly because it is much more efficient. LED lights are expensive, but they last longer than incandescent bulbs. Wind and water turbines tend to produce the more versatile AC because simple rectifiers are cheap and don't consume much energy. Converting low voltage DC to high voltage AC is a more complicated and expensive process.

Chapter 6

The Electric Conundrum

Just over 100 years ago electricity went through the "Current Wars." The Direct Current (DC) people of Thomas Edison were being challenged by the new Alternating Current (AC) people led by a Serbian immigrant named Nicola Tesla, who had quit the Edison Electric Light Co. because of this disagreement. Direct Current was the established electric supply but still relatively small—electricity was not yet the major source of energy for the home. The Edison Electric Company dominated electricity, and Edison had many patents on his electric inventions.

Since it was much more efficient to generate electricity in massive coal-fired power plants, there were few power stations and they were large and placed in densely populated areas. But it needed to be sent long distances to new customers because, at that time, almost no one had any idea of how to generate electricity. The wires taking the electricity to the consumers had "resistance"—friction that ate up much of the electric energy so you couldn't send Direct Current more than a few miles.

By 1856 it was already known that the energy loss from the resistance (friction) in wires depended exclusively on the flow rate (amperage) in the wires, not on the total energy sent (wattage). Since wattage is the product of amperage multiplied by the force (voltage) of the electricity, raising the voltage would allow you to send more energy with the same losses. How do you raise that voltage?

There was a difference between AC and DC electricity. Michael Faraday had discovered in the 1820s that moving a wire conductor through a magnetic field created an electric voltage in the wire. An electric generator (dynamo) is a device with wires on an armature, which is rotated in a powerful magnetic "field" to make electric current. That current is on the armature, so a "commutator" is required to get it into wires for general usage. The commutator sends electricity through wires from the armature directly into power lines leading to any device that needs electricity.

An alternator, on the other hand, reverses that process. The wires are in the field, and the armature is the magnet. It moves the magnetic field through the wires instead of the wires through the magnetic field. The electricity is in the field, and no commutator is needed. But the armature's magnetic field has a north pole and a south pole, so with each rotation, the current reverses as the north and south poles move past the field wires. That is alternating current (AC).

Using the same principle of moving the magnetic field instead of moving the wire, William Stanley built a "transformer." This device has two coils of wires wound around the same metallic core but insulated from each other. The coils had different numbers of loops in them so when a magnetic field moved through them, they produced different voltages. Stanley sent one voltage of alternating current through one coil (the primary coil) to create a moving magnetic field. This moving field generated a current in the other coil (the secondary coil). But since the secondary had a different number of coils, it created a different voltage. If the primary had more coils, the secondary would have a lower voltage. That's called a step-down transformer. If the primary had fewer coils, the secondary created a higher voltage—a step-up transformer. The transformer won't work on Direct Current because its magnetic field is stationary.

Nicola Tesla used William Stanley's transformers to create huge voltages of AC that could be sent many miles with minimal energy loss. The first High Tension wires were installed in 1893 and carried 2,000 volts of electricity. The High Tension wires became a basic component of "the Grid" that sent electricity to just about anywhere. Since electricity is remarkably versatile, the demand for it grew exponentially. The grid went through constant increases in voltage.

By 1914, the Grid carried 70,000 volts, which allowed long distance electric transmission. It set the stage for Franklin Roosevelt's Rural Electrification Act, which was passed by Congress in 1935. Today, they are carrying as much as 1 million volts. That is one reason why Alternating Current is entrenched, and your home is dependent upon it. That also explains why the only major DC device today is the automobile that has to store energy so it can be started. You can't store AC. You might recall that some early automobiles had a crank on the front so you could start them by turning the crank.

There are other problems with AC. If you have two sources, they must be "phased" so each peaks at the same instant. That required some standardization. National and international organizations came to separate agreements that the AC cycle should be 60 per second in North America (60 cycle) and 50 cycles per second in Europe (50 cycle). Of course, the cycles must be absolutely equal (phased) whenever two AC sources come together.

Today, we face a completely different problem. The overwhelming expansion in electric demand, particularly in the home, is for electronics. Electronics operate on low voltage DC—3, 6, or 12 volts. But our standard domestic supply from the Grid is 230/115 A/C volts. That means that we must use step-down transformers to *reduce* the voltage required to run our computers, TVs, calculators and telephones, and increasingly, our lighting. They need transformers to get their power from the Grid. Today, essentially all electronic devices have transformers either in them or on the plug that connects them to the standard electric outlet.

But lo! The solar and wind generated electricity is already low voltage DC—a perfect match for our expanding electronics industry. High voltage AC is so entrenched today that 90% of our solar and wind generated electricity is converted to high voltage and added to the Grid—another example of decisions made for profitability rather than for performance. That involves some fairly complicated and expensive equipment and consumes 2% or more of the energy being sent to the Grid. It also defeats a major reason for the use of New Energy—"alternate." When the grid is down, you are too! No energy demand should have only one source. Of course, Big Energy wants exactly the opposite—they want to be the only available energy source.

Today, if you put more energy into the Grid than you use, the electric companies are required to pay you for what you send them. So far, that is small, but it is rapidly growing. Count on it! The electric industry will fight that requirement tooth and nail. I predict that that requirement will be reduced or eliminated in a few years. Several electric companies are already trying to reduce or eliminate that requirement. The electric industry will find and promote dozens of reasons why they should not have to pay the going rate for your homemade electricity. They will point out that it is intermittent, scattered, and unpredictable. They'll claim that it will come when the demand is low instead of high. They will claim that it is unregulated and, therefore, unsafe. They will be very creative in explaining why they should not pay you for electricity. My prediction is that, politics being what it is, they will succeed. I do not recommend that you build large New Energy electric-generating systems in your home or community to capitalize on this arrangement because that will probably become wasted energy relatively soon. Generate what you need to eliminate the electric bill, but no more. If you do build large systems, do it together (**DIT**) and share it with your fellow **EnerJetts**—don't send it to Big Energy and further entrench them while giving away your backup system in case one of our increasing and more violent storms takes down some of the Grid's high tension wires.

The problem is that we currently have two different demands on our expanding electric system. They can be adjusted to work with each other, but it requires quite a lot of equipment that is fairly complex. To make them work together, you need integrators, rectifiers, phasers, and batteries. Since the voltages are not all the same, you need many transformers, and for DC batteries you need to worry about wiring them in parallel or in series. If you wire them in series, the voltage increases with each source. If you wire them in parallel, the voltage remains the same, but the amperage can increase substantially.

Since the photovoltaic and wind generated electric energy (New Energy) matches the needs of the rapidly expanding electronics industry, it would be much better to establish a separate system for Domestic Energy and feed it directly to your electronic equipment. Since the sun does not shine at night, and the wind is fickle at best, you will need a battery system to store any excess you make and to supply energy when none is being produced. It is cheaper to put in a battery system than to put in energy consuming alternators, transformers, and phasing devices to synchronize two 60 cycle sources. That also produces a great opportunity to make battery systems much more effective. Attaching our New Energy to our Old Energy system is a bonanza for the transformer manufacturer but a wasteful and complex nuisance for the user.

This is a small but growing problem. We must face the fact that there are at least two different demands for electricity today. Power equipment demands lots of energy. The Grid was created specifically to supply 240/120v AC. Electronics and communication demand low voltage and extreme mobility of electricity. Power is not a large requirement. Big Energy will want to keep you in the current system that they control. **EnerJetts**, using **DIT**, will build a large network of local New Energy systems. Remember— low voltage DC can't be sent long distances, so New Energy also means local energy. Tying New Energy to obsolete Old Energy is wasteful, expensive, and inflexible.

LED lighting, radio, TV, automobiles, computers, cell phones, and tablet users increasingly operate on low voltages. It comes free from solar, wind, tidal, and other New Energy sources. Solar and wind electricity are not ideal for running your stove, vacuum cleaner, dishwasher, or clothes dryer—those appliances were specifically designed to utilize AC power from the Grid. Most industrial electric demand is for power, not communications or calculations, so Big Energy will always have a huge market. You will not completely escape the Grid. Note that the power demand for electronics is very low. It capitalizes more on the mobility of electricity than on the power if it. Giving up electronic demand will not seriously decrease the main product Big Energy supplies—power. However, it will eliminate one of their most guarded assets—control!

It should be noted that electricity is not only a useful source of energy; it can be something of a hazard. Allowing untrained people to modify or add to this huge electric complex could indeed cause some serious problems, not only locally but throughout the system. As a result, there are regulations about the use of electric energy and particularly about adding to this massive system. If you have an electric device that you want to attach or deliver to that system, these regulations must be followed. There are a number of organizations that explain and/or control these regulations. In general, they are primarily concerned with the *safety* of and the availability of electric (and gas) energy sources. *Do not, under any circumstances, bypass or neglect these regulations.*

If you want to make any change to that system even in your own home, get a certified electrician to do it. That is not just to avoid fines for breaking the law, but for your own safety. In general, these regulations are not cumbersome and allow considerable variations in usage. They are primarily to protect you and other users of the Grid. You can find these regulations on the Internet and also many agencies that oversee and monitor them. One such agency in Montpelier, Vermont, is Regulatory Assistance Program (RAP)—raponline.org. There are many others in every state, and they are listed on the Internet under Electrical Regulatory Programs. That being said, it is much more practical to have a separate system for electronics and New Energy, rather than trying to blend them. There are essentially no serious hazards in 6, 12, or 18 volt electricity, either AC or DC.

New Energy devices produce low voltage electricity. They are not a hazard. You can put 3 or 6 volt electricity in your mouth and feel a small tingle. Don't even think about trying that with your 110 volt power from the Grid. This is why new homes need two electric systems—the domestic system from New Energy for electronics, and wires from the Grid for your washing machine and your electric stove. Don't fight Big Energy for your electricity. Work with them to put both sources to work for what they are good at.

Chapter 7

Wind

Wind is really a form of solar energy. It is the uneven heating of the earth by the sun that causes wind. It blows from cold places to warm places where the warmed air keeps rising. Wind is everywhere, but it is extremely fickle. There is a gentle breeze almost all the time almost everywhere. Violent winds blow unpredictably almost everywhere on occasion.

Windmills were first used about 200 BCE. They were used primarily to grind grain and pump water. They have seen substantial use ever since but never have been the dominant source of energy except perhaps in Holland (The Netherlands). The first windmills used to generate electricity (wind generators) were in 1887. Wind generators went through a slow and relatively small development for about 100 years, but increases in energy costs have stimulated increased development in recent years—after all, wind energy is free. Wind now supplies about 2% of the electricity in the United States and 8% in Europe.

Since wind tends to blow harder high above the ground, most wind generators are very tall—often 200 feet or more. They are located in wind corridors, on mountain tops, and on shorelines where the wind blows strongest. They tend to be large units operated by utility companies (Big Energy). Since they have to send their output long distances to the user, they usually produce high voltage AC.

Historically, electricity was generated primarily in coal-fired power plants. These tended to be large installations because the efficiency was better in larger facilities. We built large power plants in densely populated places—where the users were. They were many miles apart, so electricity often had to be sent many miles to users. As explained earlier, that required high voltage AC! When wind generators came along, we tailored them to this established pattern. That requires some fairly complex equipment that consumes some of the electric energy. That also limits the number of available sources for electricity. Big Energy loves that because they stay in control as the sole supplier. It also gives them much greater control of the prices they charge. That is the driving force behind mergers and acquisitions—to gain market control and pricing freedom.

This large high voltage demand on commercial wind generators makes them unable to operate in winds below 8 or 9 miles per hour. Even in the wind corridors that is usually less than 60% of the time. Just above your roof it is about 8% of the time. Most of the small private wind generators you see are copies of the large commercial wind generators. They must be mounted on tall poles to get up into the prevailing winds. They ignore the overwhelming majority of the wind they are supposed to be capturing and remain idle much of the time. These small local units need a completely different "wind catcher" design for local winds of 1 or 2 miles per hour.

Farm windmills originally pumped water or milled grain. That farm windmill had a completely different design for a totally different demand—much closer to the electronic demand upon today's small wind generators. There are few designs for your roof-top wind catcher designed to generate low voltage electricity and send it short distances. Manufacturers believe there isn't enough wind over your home to be worth capturing. There is some validity to that way of thinking because the energy of the wind increases not with the wind velocity, but with the square of the wind velocity. If you cut the wind velocity in half, you get 1/4 as much energy. If you cut it to a third, you get one ninth as much energy. Gentle winds carry very little energy, but they carry it all the time, and electronics don't need power so much as variability. Absolutely still air is not very common anywhere.

Today's commercial wind generators come in two basic designs—the Horizontal Axis Wind Turbine (HAWT) and the Vertical Axis Wind Turbine (VAWT). In general, the HAWT is not really a turbine but is somewhere between a propeller and the farm windmill. They tend to have three to six blades set at an angle to the incoming wind. They capture its energy to drive a generator contained inside its hub. Unlike a solar panel, they have the flexibility to generate a variety of electric outputs. They can make AC or DC in a wide variety of voltages depending upon the generator they drive. They need to face the wind to operate, so they have a fin or tail to keep them facing the wind. This requirement gave rise to the VAWT, which operates when the wind blows from any direction—no fin or tail is needed. The VAWT is much less efficient than the HAWT merely because the blades have to return against the very wind that drives them.

Highly complex blade designs minimize this problem, and some operate quite effectively in all winds. There are two common types of VAWT. Some have curved blades arranged in some sort of a corkscrew format, often tapered toward the top. Others are cylindrical collections of flat or slightly tapered slats that swivel to keep them catching the incoming wind but turning to avoid the same wind in the return path. There are other variations on these themes, and Vertical Axis Wind Turbines demonstrate quite a lot of creativity in design. Many can be found on the Internet. They come with detailed explanations of why each design is better than its competitors for their various optimum wind conditions.

Few wind turbines on the market today operate in the low winds that surround your home. Since that is where the electricity is used and where the winds are, new designs for that purpose are needed. Few companies believe that gentle wind is worth capturing, but it is over 70% of all wind energy below 200 feet from the ground.

There are many wind generators on the market today. Your **EnerJett** group can study and assess these on the Internet to find which local sources provide the most cost-effective designs for your wind conditions before you buy or build them. I suspect that you will be disappointed if you are looking for wind generators that work in winds from 1 to 8 mph. Such designs exist, and some can be found on the Internet. They may not be commercially available in your area. Evaluating their performance versus your specific needs is a complex study and may be beyond many users. **DIT** opportunity for **EnerJetts**?

There has not been a lot of design creativity in HAWTs. They are pretty much windmills with from 3 to 12 blades. They all have fins to keep them facing the wind, but there is not a lot of flexibility in the airfoil design to increase its efficiency. I am surprised to find that the shape of the blade seems to be rather rigid because that could present some real changes in the amount of energy they are able to extract from flowing air of different energies. Most seem to be aimed at the higher wind velocities where turbulence is a substantial factor in the flow of the air through the blade assembly. At lower velocities, which most designers tend to ignore, there is room for lots of creativity to maximize the output. They appear to think that it is not worth their while. Besides, most designers are aiming at the large commercial market rather than domestic energy. But domestic energy is 1/3 of our total demand. It has not lent itself to massive corporations because both the wind energy and the users are essentially everywhere.

There is another unused possibility for wind generators. Many of our most efficient air blowers are truly turbines. These have cylindrical squirrel cages constructed of many narrow blades that capture the air as they rotate and drive it out an exit. If you reverse that and push wind through the device, you can generate electricity instead of consuming it. They are remarkably efficient in air movement because they don't need to stop the wind to capture its energy. They can indeed be used to capture the energy of wind. In fact, they have another advantage—they can be either HAWT or VAWT devices. They may even be able to surpass the Betz calculated maximum available (59%) of the energy entering windmills. To my knowledge, there aren't any on the market, and I find no plans for **DIT**ers. (I have developed and patented the Light Wind Generator for winds from 1 to 8 mph. It should be on the market soon.)

Your New Energy takes a different point of view. It wants to capitalize on the fact that the available wind energy is scattered in the same manner as the users—everywhere. Small (3 to 5 feet diameter) units can supply substantial portions of your electric demand free of charge. I see this as an opportunity to create a huge cottage industry in the world. Your **EnerJett** group should be able to build and install one for between $200 and $400. Energy is already the largest industry, and it is perfectly suited to capitalize on local small winds that are everywhere. In the U.S., there is also a mass of unemployed, factory-trained workers who would love to build, install, and maintain their neighborhood wind generators, solar panels, and geothermal systems. Your

EnerJett group might want to help pay for a training course or program in alternate energy installation for some of those unemployed or underemployed factory worker neighbors.

The placement of the roof-top wind generator is fairly critical to maximizing its output. Most roofs are in neighborhoods or groups. That tends to block or hinder the wind. But just above this stagnant space there is a small layer of greater flow where all the wind that was blocked below flows. Obviously, you want to capitalize on this fairly consistent pattern. Depending upon the surrounding terrain, the layer of increased flow can be anywhere from 2 feet to 20 feet above the chosen structure.

In some instances, it will change depending upon the wind direction and the surrounding structures. In those areas, your **EnerJett** chapter should find the prime direction of the prevailing winds and capitalize on that wind configuration. Wind indicators are not as hard to find as are the people who will climb the roofs and measure the wind patterns there. In general, the maximum wind energy will be higher rather than lower, although certain peaked roofs that are perpendicular to the prevailing wind may create a channel fairly close to the peak of the roof.

The mounting of the wind generator is also critical. Since they will usually be the highest thing in their area, they are also an attraction for lightning. Minimize the metal content of the device. Blades and the tail or fin should be weatherproofed wood or plastic rather than metal. Mounting poles should be plastic rather than metal, and guy-wires should be fabric (clothes line?). Think replaceable rather than durable. The wires to the structure below should be enclosed in the plastic mounting pole. If the exposure is severe, it may well require a lightning rod to protect it. And remember—the commonest complaint about rooftop windmills is their noise. Keeping them in plastic or wood and mounting them on a closed-cell foam foot should eliminate or minimize any sound pollution. The same practices that limit their attractiveness to lightning also minimize their sound transmission.

Wind generated electricity can be either AC or DC, unlike photovoltaic energy, which is only DC. More electronics devices use DC rather than AC, but converting AC to DC is relatively simple with a rectifier. AC generators need no brushes. Brushes are small carbon contacts that conduct the generated DC electricity from the generator shaft to the electric circuit it is supplying. AC generators need no such brushes since their electricity is generated in the field coil, not the armature. They have fewer maintenance problems and greater freedom of rotation. They will work in slightly lower wind velocities because there is less friction on the rotating armature.

New Energy is everywhere, so it is adaptable to small units for local demands, as well as massive facilities to serve industry. This is a reason to view commercial and domestic energy separately. **EnerJetts** tend to serve domestic energy demands that are small and locally scattered. Commercial demands tend to be large and more distantly dispersed. Everything about light wind favors the creation of many small units for specific local purposes rather than massive supplies for large areas. Really big winds are destructive, and neither system makes much use of them, but each needs safety features to protect them. That is why working *with* Big Energy is best. It removes some of the expansion demand on Big Energy and eliminates much long distance transportation of energy. Most of the principles apply to both, but variations in the approach will help Big Energy satisfy the bulk of its big customer base while allowing **EnerJetts** to serve their local customers with low voltage. **DIT** works! Unlike those massive windmills you see on the mountains, small wind generators (wind catchers) have curved blades that are wider at the tips and capture the light winds that assail them.

Chapter 8

Geothermal Energy

The core of the earth is hot—about 5700° K (9300° F). That is because much of our earth contains unstable radioactive elements (those with atomic numbers above 86) that slowly break down and produce heat when they do. The earth's center is 4,000 miles away, so that heat dissipates as it slowly escapes the earth. At about 10 feet below the frost line, it is a constant 55° F on solid earth everywhere. 55° F is not a comfortable temperature for most of us, but it is a gigantic source of heat energy. We have learned to make refrigerants—liquids that boil below 55° F and become gases. Those gases are very mobile and can be compressed and piped from one location to another. Compressing a gas increases its temperature, so these hot gases are used to deliver heat to buildings or machinery. This is called geothermal heating. It is remarkably stable and consistent, so it has enormous potential for heating homes and water. It is essentially unlimited, so it has tremendous potential for the whole world.

But it takes quite a lot of area to absorb enough heat to keep a building warm, so excavation is a major expense of geothermal heating and cooling facilities. Drilling down to this heat source can be quite expensive, so geothermal energy systems are not cheap to install. However, their productivity is large because by reversing the process, they can also cool homes in the hot summer. They are also used to heat water. Despite their large, up-front cost, geothermal systems can have payback periods under three years. Please also note that this is not quite free energy as are solar and wind energy. You need to install pipes to bring the refrigerant to the compressor. The refrigerant gas is compressed to heat it up and sent through a heat exchanger to deliver the heat to its destination. You need electric power to compress the refrigerant and to pump it to where it is needed. That is also true of the reverse process for cooling homes in the hot summer. This energy demand is about 1/5 to 1/3 of the energy delivered, but it is a requirement. I suspect development can reduce that cost to less than 20%.

Geothermal systems have limitations as well as opportunities. There are three basic components to a geothermal HVAC (Heating, Ventilating, and Air Conditioning) system. First, there is the network of pipes (usually plastic) containing fluids that move the energy to the refrigerant compressor. This is referred to as the "earth loop." It is buried in the earth where the temperature is 55° F. It must be at least 10 feet deep to absorb the steady warmth you seek, so excavation is required, and the area is often quite large. If you are in a dense city area, finding open fields to accommodate your loop is often quite a problem. The answer is sometimes just to drill deeper instead of digging up acres of ground. You also need a compressor to compress and heat those refrigerant gases and pump them to the heat exchanger. Finally, you need a pump to send the heat into the structure to be heated. Planning is clearly a critical requirement.

You can find geothermal conversion systems on the Internet, but make sure you are only buying what you need instead of some fancy equipment that increases the cost of installation. You can purchase such units, but **DIT** may be quite a challenge for amateurs. They are not cheap and are rarely a **DIY** project. Using your local skills, your **EnerJett** group can usually get the job done. Be sure to check with the local town ordinances to be sure there aren't restrictions on digging.

Often there are already underground pipes, sewers, or wires that must not be disturbed. Be sure to run your payback period calculations before you take on such a costly project. If your payback is over 5 years, be very cautious. Be sure to determine if joint operations for two or more homes could be more cost effective.

There is another opportunity, much like that of solar shingles. On new homes or apartment buildings, substantial excavation is usually required to establish the basement and foundation for the new structure. Capitalize on that, and plan ahead. Why not use that same excavation process to make room for an earth loop? Install the loop under the basement or foundation. Unfortunately, the area beneath a structure is rarely enough to provide enough heat to keep it warm, but it can supply a substantial portion of it. Excavation can also go beyond the foundation or go deep beneath it. In any event, this minimizes the most costly feature of geothermal systems. I envision the basements of all new homes having geothermal earth loops under them because tradition already requires that we have a foundation and usually a basement for new structures. This obviously will not apply to existing homes where the foundations are already in place. But beware! Big Energy will oppose such actions and will doubtless try to pass laws prohibiting geothermal loops under basements. Each such unit represents loss of a customer to Big Energy.

I would like to see state laws requiring earth loops under all new basements and foundations. That could be a large step toward energy independence and the end of climate change and global warming. I suspect that states north of the Mason Dixon line (39°N) will find this idea more attractive than those in southern climates, but it applies to every state.

Chapter 9

Tesla Free Energy

I mentioned earlier that we are not using all of the sun's radiated energy. There is a massive one in particular that has been neglected. This is not because we didn't know about it, but because it threatened the establishment. Big Energy fought ferociously to suppress it. I call it Tesla Free Energy because Nicola Tesla discovered it around 1890 and figured out how to use it. He was bitterly opposed by Big Energy because they thought that it could completely overwhelm their market. There was a good deal of truth in this belief, so they not only suppressed this system, they lied about it, spending hours and much venom to discredit Tesla and keep his knowledge from the public. In fact, his laboratory and all his work were burned down in 1895. There is no proof, but it is probable that the fire was deliberately set. Big Energy considered his ideas a serious threat to their monopoly and even to their existence.

What is this mysterious energy source? Quite simply, it is magnetism. Earth is a large magnet. We are all engulfed in a weak magnetic field that originates deep within the earth. This is the energy that drives compasses. Without it, early navigators could, and did, get easily lost. That is why world exploration was rare and risky before about 1100 CE when the magnetic compass was first understood. Its first use as a ships navigational tool was in 1405 by a Chinese sailor named Zeng He. That is why Columbus had few predecessors of significance. Using a magnetic compass, Columbus thought he was taking a short route to China but discovered instead that the earth was about twice as large as previously believed. What he found was North America. (Actually, he found the island of Hispaniola, which is now Haiti and the Dominican Republic.) There were (naked) people living there. He could easily see that these people weren't Chinese, so he believed he had arrived in India instead of China. So he called those people Indians. It is clear that Columbus did not discover America. He just found a successful way for Europeans to get there. Native Americans (American Indians) had already been living there for centuries.

What Nicola Tesla discovered was that the sun has a similar magnetic field. It is substantially larger than the earth's magnetic field, but we are 93 million miles from the sun, so at our distance it is roughly equal in strength to the earth's magnetism. But, unlike the earth's magnetism, and unknown to Tesla at the time, the sun's magnetic field is not static; it changes on a regular schedule. In fact, it reverses about every 13 years. It did so in 2014/2015.

Tesla knew that moving an electric conductor (wire) through a magnetic field creates an electric voltage (discovered by Michael Faraday in 1831). He figured that wires on Earth were all moving through the sun's magnetic field and were undoubtedly having electric voltage driven into them, but at the time, no one knew how to make use of that voltage, which they didn't even know was there. The few people who understood that didn't concern themselves about it because the sun's magnetic field was weak. They had already designed electric generators that used man-made magnets many times as strong as the sun's or the earth's magnetic fields. Besides, how do you capture that solar energy and make it useful? If you put up a loop, one side of the loop will drive electricity in one direction, and the other side of that loop will drive it in the same direction. In a loop, they will oppose each other and we get no electric current. It requires some careful configurations to capture and use that electric current. People at that time had no idea of how to do that—but Tesla did.

The amount of voltage created in a conductor moving through a magnetic field depends not only upon the strength of the magnetic field, but upon the speed at which the conductor moves through it. To get a little technical, the voltage derives from the number of magnetic lines of force it cuts through each second. The sun's magnetic field here on Earth is small—few magnetic lines of force. But the velocity is enormous! We are moving through the sun's magnetic field at 83,000 feet per second—twelve times as fast as the fastest bullet we have ever been able to make commercially. Tesla figured out (and patented) how to capture and use that electric force. He invented a Tesla coil (there are several Tesla coils) in 1893 that captured the magnetic energy of the sun.

Very few people understood this phenomenon, and most people thought it was a hoax. Big Energy did understand and knew it could be a universal source of electricity. That drove them wild. How could they sell electricity to people who had all they needed right in their own home? They tried to invalidate his patent and publicly ridiculed its "crazy" inventor. He was indeed an odd-ball, and quite a showman, displaying huge sparks and arcs to impress the public. But he was probably one of the most productive geniuses who ever lived. It is reported that Big Energy even murdered some of Tesla's workers and cohorts. It is probable that it was they who burned down his laboratory. Tesla died in 1943 a discredited pauper, and his Tesla coil had never found public usage. If Big Energy has its way, it never will!

To this day, most people believe that the Tesla coil is a hoax, or at best, a trick. Big Energy encourages such disbelief. They are assisted by the fact that building a Tesla coil is beyond the comprehension of most people. They don't understand exactly what they are trying to do. It is interesting to note that I have never seen in writing a clear explanation of this magnetic potential. I presume that is primarily because of Big Energy's embargo. This is probably the largest unused source of energy on Earth, and eventually we will use it despite Big Energy's opposition. The surprising thing is that Big Energy could also use it to increase their profit margins because the product they sell would cost them nothing. They don't. You won't learn it from Big Energy, nor from the schools that Big Energy subsidizes.

Nicola's patent expired in 1910 and finds little attention today. It is real and does indeed produce useable electricity. It is a massive force through which the earth and all its contents are moving every minute of every day. It could be the largest source of electricity in the world. It lends itself to millions of small generators rather than a few massive ones. No wonder Big Energy hates it.

There are no Tesla free-energy systems on the market today. That is primarily because of Big Energy's embargo. But you can find and purchase plans on the Internet, build one for under $300, and get free electricity for the rest of your life. Be careful, however. The plans on the Internet never explain exactly what you are doing. Since the technology was under rigid opposition by Big Energy, most of them are sub rosa schemes that claim to be simple but aren't really. There are far more scams out there than actual plans for a productive electric generator. Some of them actually do work, but finding them is a challenge. Consider the Hendershot Generator, or the Power Innovator program, but be very cautious. Your **EnerJett** group can be of great assistance in this **DIT** project. It might be easier if two or three of you got together and built one for each of you. You could learn from each other and enjoy the process together. You can teach your unemployed factory workers to build them and supply your whole neighborhood. **Energettics.com** has some information and would love to help. But beware of potential lawsuits. Big Energy vehemently opposes to any Tesla energy projects.

One amazing fact is that the Public Utilities do not see this as an opportunity for them as well. After U.S. Patent #512,340 expired in 1910, they could well use the Tesla coil on a massive scale and get free electricity to sell to an uninformed (or misinformed) public. There has been essentially no effort on this. That is something of a mystery, which I suspect is related more to profitability of the coal and oil companies who supply 80% of our electric energy. Since coal is our worst polluter, that tells us a lot about a Public Utility that makes decisions based on profitability instead of public interest. I suspect that, even in the electric industry, many people really believe that the Tesla coil is a hoax. They have been telling the world that for over 100 years. Many of the explanations of the Tesla coil I have seen claim that we are capitalizing on the earth's magnetism. That is wrong. It is the magnetic energy of the sun. The earth's magnetism moves with the earth and is not a source of induced electricity because we are not moving through it.

This problem leads to the conclusion that we should consider having two different sources of electricity because there are two widely different uses for it. Historically, we have used electricity primarily for power and for lighting. But electronics have a completely different demand for electricity. Low voltage is the name of the game in electronics because miniaturization is critical to its progress. Small things have thin insulators, and high voltages arc right through them. Higher voltage was the name of the game in power demands of both industrial and home use. But incandescent lighting is inefficient, and the new LED (Light Emitting Diodes) lighting is tending toward low voltage and much higher efficiency. Lighting is headed toward electronics in its demand. It is time we recognized the dual nature of electricity and capitalize on the sources that satisfy each.

Small Tesla coils could and should be a major source of electricity throughout the world. They are not expensive and present no additional hazard to the user. I'm sure that they can be abused, as is almost every advanced technical development at some point, but it is a truly massive potential source of free electricity. I suspect and believe that it will become a major energy source in the next 40 years. If we work *with* Big Energy instead of fighting them, that can become a reality within your lifetime. Domestic energy is only 1/3 of the total energy demand. If we encourage Tesla coils in domestic energy, that will relieve some upgrading pressure on Big Energy and allow them to invest their money in New Energy and increase their profitability. Your teenage kids can probably build one, but I strongly recommend that you get an electrician to connect it to any electric appliances or supply. That is probably a requirement in most communities.

There could be some real hazards in uncontrolled electricity in the hands of amateurs.

There are several sources of information on Tesla coils and how to build and use them. Big Energy despises them and does what it can to keep them off the market. Most are available in clandestine emails that are often shut down. This encourages scam artists who are interested in making money rather than in providing cheaper electricity. There are good plans out there and I suspect there will soon be actual Tesla Generators on the market, but that will probably be a slow process considering Big Energy's opposition. **EnerJett** opportunity?

Chapter 10

New Hydro Energy

There are rivers and streams almost everywhere. These channels carry rain water back to the oceans from which it evaporated. Considering that the evaporation of ocean water to form clouds, rain, and snow is the largest energy transfer system in the world, it is no surprise that it carries massive amounts of energy with it. What is a surprise is that there are only seven major hydroelectric facilities in the U.S. The world's first major hydroelectric facility was Niagara Falls in 1897, culminating in the Grand Coulee Dam, which was the world's largest when it went on stream in 1942.

We tend to think in terms of large facilities, but in fact there is more energy in the small streams and rivers than there is in those big power stations. It is indeed scattered around, but so are the users! There are many recent improvements in water turbines that could make small facilities practical sources of local energy. The nice thing about these installations is that they work 365 days a year. The flow may vary considerably, but it is always there. The surprising thing about this is that there are very few small water turbine generators on the market today. I know of no American company that is building them.

To generate electricity from flowing water traditionally has required two factors: flow rate and head (head is the distance the water drops to gain momentum). Most hydroelectric facilities of any size establish reservoirs of water and feed it down through gates and locks to drive electric generators. Since these are large facilities, they are not usually near heavily populated areas of high demand. Few of us live next to Niagara Falls. Our response has been to make hydroelectric power in high voltage Alternating Current (AC) that can be shipped long distances. So far, we have ignored the opportunity to generate low voltage for local use. But the explosive new demand for electric energy is primarily for electronics—low voltage Direct Current (DC). In addition, batteries can store DC but not AC.

The electronics demand is not so much for power as it is for electron mobility and activity. The electron is the most mobile and flexible energy source in the universe. It is ideal for communications, data storage, and complex electronics equipment. That makes the demand better satisfied by small local sources instead of massive ones that send huge power many miles to massive recipients. There are streams in almost every town in the world. Streams were often the reason for locating the communities where they are. These streams can and should be used to power the local computer, tablet, or cell phone. They aren't! Primarily because it is difficult to create a head that is powerful enough to drive machinery to generate electricity.

Since few people or communities want to build or live with a giant water wheel, I was surprised to find that there are very few small hydroelectric turbines or water wheels on the market—the ones that require no head. There are quite a few larger hydropower units on the market. Most are made outside the United States—in China, Turkey, Italy, or Australia. We are missing a huge opportunity. Small hydroelectric units could be extremely effective in small towns on streams everywhere. They can even be used for individual homes that are adjacent to a stream or river. Since about 2005, there have been quite a number of small water-driven generators put on the market. These one to five kilowatt units can supply enough electricity for a household. I don't think any of them is American. One of them, PowerSpout, is an Australian generator that comes in a variety of small units from around $800 to about $2,000. You can get details on the web at www.powerspout.com. Another is New Energy Corp. in Victoria, Canada (www.newenergycorp.ca). They have units from 2KW to 25 KW. There are several others, but they are not advertised and are often difficult to find. Your **EnerJett** group can find them.

We have some outdated thinking about most of our hydroelectric power. It is pretty obvious that waterfalls and falling water carry substantial energy because of their head, but we ignore the less dramatic flowing water that moves the vast majority of our rainfall to the oceans. Worldwide, rivers and streams move more water than waterfalls. After all, the flow of water is driven by the ubiquitous gravity. They are just less impressive. Because of this most commercial water-driven generators require a head to operate—we tend to overlook the gentle flowing of rivers and streams. But they are scattered everywhere and can provide energy to remote areas and neighborhoods.

If we placed water wheels or turbines along those rivers and streams, we could draw substantial energy from them without damaging anyone or anything. You might want to put a conical open-mesh screen on the turbine inlet to keep out fish and debris because leaves and debris are the largest barriers to their operation. PowerSpout has solved that problem. New Energy Corporation has designed a system that requires no head—it uses the power of the flowing water in the river or stream. Once installed, they produce free energy for local use. No massive facility is needed, and we need not send the output hundreds of miles to the user. We are talking hundreds of dollars, not millions of dollars, to install these power sources. Not every neighborhood is on a stream, but a great many are. It is worthy to note that they can also be used to capture the energy of incoming and receding tides along ocean shores (See chapter 11).

There are a few water generators of advanced design available on the open market. Your **EnerJetts** could put a dozen or so along a stream and do no damage to anyone. The cost is relatively minor, and the payback period is often less than a year. In northern climates, they will often work even under the ice that forms on the surface. Almost no streams completely freeze during winter. Even if they do, why throw away the rest of the year's bounty? No one owns any river or stream, but those streams often flow on privately owned property, so some negotiation with the landowners may be required. This should not be difficult, since the landowner will be a prime beneficiary of the electric output. He might even become an **EnerJett**.

Early water wheels were massive structures. They were quite popular until the discovery of coal and oil brought the cost of energy down dramatically. They were not used to generate electricity until after 1900. Then they were redesigned and made much smaller and more practical. Today, they are hardly used for anything else. Few hydroelectric facilities were built between the WWI and WWII, but the dramatic increase in fossil fuel prices in the 1970s made coal-fired power plants more costly than hydroelectric power. We began building more hydroelectric facilities. There are about 2000 small hydroelectric power plants in the U.S. Today, about 8% of U.S. electric power is from hydroelectric sources and nearly 20% worldwide.

Your **EnerJett** group can find the local sources and the local demand to determine the most cost-effective way to supply energy needed within the community. Then their job is to organize local people so that they *want* to get the job done. Set goals and schedules. Have target dates, and give rewards for jobs well done. Work with other nearby **EnerJett** groups, and you might even compete with them for specific targets. Have completion parties.

Encourage new ideas on how to save energy or how to improve performance, or find new ways to get things done. Unlike solar panels, water turbines and water generators can generate either AC or DC. If you find a new idea that helps your group, post it on **Energettics.com.** You not only learn from **Energettics.com**, you help it get better day by day.

Hydropower is an example of the value of **Doing It Together**. Hydropower also adapts to moderate-sized facilities that are too big for a single home but perfect for a neighborhood. Together, **EnerJetts** can accomplish projects for the whole neighborhood. Here is a perfect opportunity to meet, work with, and enjoy your neighbors on a community project.

Chapter 11

Lunar Energy

The moon weighs about 1.2% as much as the earth. It has substantial gravity that affects us on Earth 243,000 miles away. The most obvious result is the tides we see in our oceans twice every day. In fact, we have daily tides of about 6 inches in the solid ground under our feet. But it is the ocean tides that capture our attention and present a reliable source of energy that we learned how to use over a thousand years ago. People built "barrages" in tidal basins to capture flood tides and drain the ebbing tide through water wheels used primarily to grind grain and pump fresh water. There is evidence of the use of tidal power for grinding grain into flour before 900 CE, but records are sketchy and somewhat vague.

Tidal technology has been largely neglected for centuries. It was not until after WWII that technological advances were applied to tidal power. In 1966, France built a 240 Megawatt tidal power station on the Rance River at St. Malo. South Korea is building a 254 MW (the world's largest) tidal power station on Sihwa Bay. It is still under construction but is already producing power. There is another 240 MW power plant on Swansea Bay in the UK. There is also a 16 Megawatt tidal station at Annapolis, Nova Scotia. There are others, but most of them are smaller. They tend to be used for domestic power rather than industrial power. There are only seven major tidal power stations worldwide despite the fact that the new water turbines they use are remarkably efficient. Nine more are planned, and one is already under construction. They are becoming ever more popular. There is substantial interest and development of tidal power, and advanced technical developments are creating opportunities for massive use of tides. The natural configuration of our oceans produces many more such opportunities in Europe and Asia than in North America. There are none in the United States today. Usable tides are distributed unevenly all around the earth.

There are indeed some problems with tidal generators. They tend to disrupt the local ecology of tidal basins and actually kill substantial numbers of migratory fish. They also impede local boating traffic if they are not carefully designed. Environmental groups have filed lawsuits against some of the tidal proposals, and the development of safe configurations is still underway. It seems unlikely that massive industrial tidal barrages will become commonplace, but smaller ones that cater to the local communities may well become very common. Newer technology can produce major increases in tidal power. Barrages capture the energy of receding tides from tidal basins, but newer configurations can capture the energy of the incoming tides as well as the receding tides, doubling their energy output.

Tidal energy is a good example of our ossified thinking. We make plans for massive power stations on tidal basins, but there are almost no small stations that serve shoreline communities. Since tides occur on every coastline, there are hundreds of opportunities for small community-based tidal stations. All you need is a suitable water wheel or turbine and a little planning. That is particularly suitable for your **EnerJett** group because tidal power is even more adaptable to towns and neighborhoods rather than to the individual home. Most tidal basins are small and lend themselves to local usage rather than massive energy sources to be sent miles away to users. There is an enormous amount of available energy in those tides, but we have not yet solved all the problems they can cause. Can your **EnerJett** group?

Consider this. Many of the beaches and shorelines around the world are protected by "breakwaters." These are small rock walls built under water from 30 to 300 feet offshore. They were built to control the tidal flow around beaches and shorelines. Why not put waterwheel generators about every five feet along these breakwaters and wire them to the local population? They will generate quite a lot of electricity when the tide comes in. Then they will generate about the same amount as the tide goes out. This is obviously a community project and would be perfect for your local **EnerJett** group. Water is fairly heavy stuff and carries quite a lot of energy as it moves. Tides move immense quantities of water and can deliver massive amounts of energy. It is not as prevalent as air and wind, but flowing water weighs 800 times as much as air, so it carries much more energy. To be sure, tides are intermittent, but they are on a regular schedule that is mapped and reported for all to see. Building small tidal pools near the mouth of streams and rivers can capture a great deal of energy that is completely ignored today. **DIT** opportunity?

Chapter 12

Batteries

One of the problems with New Energy is that it is almost always intermittent. The wind does not blow all the time, and the sun doesn't shine at night. Since demand is continuous, there is a requirement for providing energy when the source is not operative. Wind and sun may deliver more energy than is needed right now, but when they stop, we still need energy. The storage battery was invented in France by Gaston Planté in 1859. It was basically the lead-acid battery that you use in your automobile today. It will store excess electric energy in productive times and supply needed energy in idle times.

Batteries became pretty basic after their improvement by Antoine Fauré in 1881. Until recently, there have been no major changes but many small improvements, so their performance has increased. They did the job so well that there has been relatively little effort to improve them until very recently. The electronic era has increased the demand for small storage batteries as well as substantial improvements in size and performance. The intermittent nature of New Energy has stimulated great advances in battery technology just since the year 2000. There are many very efficient batteries on the market today in a large variety of sizes and voltages, although 3 and 6 volt batteries dominate the small battery market because that is the demand in electronics.

You might wonder why electronics favors low voltages. Electronic devices all need some sort of storage device to keep data and programs available. But there is great pressure to make these devices small and portable. You can't take your desktop computer on the subway to work every day. As you shrink the size of these devices, the insulation required to keep the electricity where you want it becomes ever thinner and smaller. But thin insulation can't contain high voltage—it arcs right through it. So as miniaturization became ever more prevalent, voltages kept going down to prevent the arcing destruction of tiny devices. 3 and 6 volt devices are common.

The creativity that allowed us to make tablets can still be applied to batteries for New Energy in the home. These tend to be the size of automobile batteries and may well be substantially more efficient because of recent developments. Also, the advent of hybrid and electric vehicles has put heavy pressure on battery development. Nonetheless, batteries that store your New Energy during prolific times are an important factor in going clean and free. And remember, putting your New Energy on the Grid" eliminates a prime reason for New Energy—an alternate in case of failure.

There are three types of batteries for home energy systems: the lead acid battery, like your automobile battery, the gel battery, and the Absorbed Glass Matt battery. They all come primarily with 6 to 18 volt output. The lead-acid battery has a problem in your home. It produces hydrogen gas when it is charged and needs to be vented if kept indoors. It costs about $100 per Kilowatt Hour (KWH) of storage capacity. It has a life expectancy of over ten years. The gel battery produces no hydrogen when charging and can be used indoors where the temperature is more constant and the battery life longer. They range about $125/

KWH of storage capacity. They will outlast the lead-acid battery. The Absorbed Glass Mat battery is relatively new and advanced—it was developed primarily for solar panels. It costs about $150 per KWH of storage capacity. They will presumably last many years—substantially more than either the lead acid or the gel battery.

All batteries of any type will last longer and perform better if they are not overstrained. If your house uses 5 KWH of stored energy on a regular basis, you should have a 10 KWH battery, so it is rarely below 50% charged.

Chapter 13

Recovering

We have been seriously polluting our world for several centuries. So far, *Your New Energy* has dealt with creative ways to stop both further pollution and energy cost increases. But what can we do about the damage we have already done? We added 540 billion tons of prehistoric carbon dioxide to our atmosphere just in the past century. Our conservation measures may stop further increases, but what do we do about that old carbon we have already added—and about the climate damage it has already caused?

Nature has provided a few solutions that we tend to ignore—in fact, we are destroying them. Trees and vegetation take carbon dioxide out of our atmosphere and create living matter out of it, using the energy of sunlight. Trees and forests are a massive air cleaning system. We have cut down half of the world's forests and are busy cutting down more. This is a formula for disaster. It disrupts the million-year-old balance between carbon producing animals and carbon consuming plants—the balance that created all of today's life. We feel the consequences every day with increased storms, rain, and energy costs as we decrease the availability of fossil fuels and make them harder to access.

There are many serious results from our profligacy. Carbon dioxide is a sunlight absorber. As we increase the carbon in our atmosphere, it warms up. In the last century, we have increased the temperature of our world and our atmosphere 2° F and the moisture content of our air by 9%. Our oceans have risen almost a foot and may well increase another 8 feet because of the melting of the Arctic and Antarctic ice caps. We have increased the acidity of our oceans by almost 30% and seriously strained much marine life. I hesitate to mention the masses of plastic and garbage that we have deposited in our oceans, but I do not hesitate to mention that burning coal has quintupled the mercury content of our atmosphere and our oceans. Mercury compounds are extremely toxic and pose serious hazards to living creatures, particularly marine species. We have no idea how many land animals we have stressed biologically like we have done to the marine species. Do you think a 40% increase in the vital atmospheric carbon dioxide can be completely ignored by plants and animals?

This is not a tale of gloom. There are things that we can do right now to restore our world. Since trees are the largest single air cleaner on Earth, let's give them a boost. I propose **ArborClean**—a program for our public schools. Every K-12 student should plant a tree-sapling on Arbor Day every year. That is about 50 million trees in the U.S. every year. It is also 50 million students who gain a little understanding of our energy dilemma. Yes, it will be quite a strain for our teachers to find places to put those trees in the inner city, but isn't that what education is all about? Even teachers can learn! Parents can volunteer spaces in their yards for new trees. Schoolyards can have trees. Shopping malls can provide space for trees around their parking lots. We can add trees to our parks and walking trails. Most towns have crews that are charged with keeping trees and vegetation throughout their jurisdiction. Schools can work with them to identify places that need trees. This might even be an opportunity for some of your older students (grades 10-12) to get involved with the planning as well as the planting. Where do you get 50 million saplings every year? Consider the **UrbanAg** (Urban Agriculture) project, described in the next chapter.

I suspect that a large part of this is in our education system. Where do our young people learn to throw garbage out of their car windows or drop pop bottles on the sidewalk? Have you seen the tons of trash that line our highways? That didn't grow there. Did any teacher ever tell you that trash containers are deliberately placed everywhere and there is no need to throw trash in front of whoever comes behind you? Just the trash floating on our oceans is calculated to be larger than the Hawaiian Islands. Whales and tuna fish didn't put that there. Perhaps we should consider setting aside a few large container ships and have them on continual trash collecting journey. Putting a recycling charge on bottles and cans could help pay for that project. If you turn in your container, you get credit on your recycling charge.

Our recent trend toward recycling should include the simple process of using our existing disposal system instead of abandoning and neglecting the myriad containers we use but don't consume. I don't blame the schools so much as the fact that we have increased our population so greatly that disposal is a major problem that didn't even concern us 100 years ago. It is interesting to note that the world (and American) population has tripled in my lifetime. If we continue that, the earth will be uninhabitable in about 100 years.

I have a crazy idea. I think that our police should issue pollution tickets to any vehicle that throws trash out the window onto the highway. The punishment is not a fine, but 5 hours of clean up duty collecting trash off of public places. Or perhaps a few days aboard one of those trash boats. I hesitate to put them on the highways where it is needed most because of the serious hazard of having untrained people walking beside heavy traffic. They can clean up the city street gutters, sidewalks, and parks. They can clean up our beaches. That forces me to admit to a habit I have developed. I love apples. I do throw apple cores out my car window. They are biodegradable and contain apple seeds. I am happy to plant apple trees along our highways.

Much of this problem is merely lack of education. People who toss cans, bottles, and plastic cups out of their moving cars don't even think about the problems they cause. Of course, we should teach conservation in our schools. McDonald's and Wendy's should put warnings on their containers as well as providing trash containers at their stores. They might even offer a free burger or soda to people who can fill a special container with discarded trash from the surrounding area. (The town or state should offer tax relief for such actions.) Should we consider a "disposal tax" on all metal, plastic, and waxed paper food containers? Your **EnerJett** group can devise special incentives for your local area.

Living things are not the only things that come from carbon dioxide. Carbon dioxide is a reactive chemical that reacts with many things to form carbonates. There are many useful products that are carbonates. What we need is some creative thinking on your part to devise some carbonate products that can be formed from the carbon dioxide in the atmosphere. I had the crazy idea of making synthetic marble—a beautiful form of calcium carbonate. The problem is that the lime needed to react with the atmospheric carbon dioxide is not naturally occurring. It requires the heating of limestone to form the lime needed to make the marble by cooking off its carbon dioxide. So all you are doing is taking the carbon dioxide out of limestone and returning it in your marble factory—there is no gain and lots of expense. Hopefully you could devise a better plan and another carbonate product that is useful in large quantities. Where else can you make a useful carbonate product from the carbon in the air? We need your ideas! Our trees need your help!

Carbon recycling is not limited to trees. Any green plant absorbs carbon dioxide from the atmosphere. The recent green trend of putting greenery on the roofs of city buildings is a wonderful move in the right direction (See the chapter on **UrbanAg**). There are many opportunities to plant greenery. Consider the U.S. Highway System. Why not plant bushes, shrubs, or even vegetables in the center strips of our major highways? Could that be a source of saplings for the **ArborGreen** project? With all the carbon-spewing vehicles whizzing by, they will certainly have a rich source of their main food. I'm not too pleased with looking at oncoming lights of vehicles at night. Bushes and shrubs in the center strip could eliminate much of that. It might even eliminate much mowing expense.

Chapter 14

UrbanAg—Greening our Cities

You'd be amazed by how many flat-top buildings there are in our cities. Thousands of acres that were grass 150 years ago are now bare-top buildings in our inner cities. Urban Agriculture (**UrbanAg**) plants gardens on those roofs. They install flats with 8 or 10 inches of gardening mulch instead of the much heavier garden soil. Existing roofs will support that growing medium. Here, we plant vegetables that are climate selected to the location. For saplings, shrubs, or deeper vegetables like potatoes or carrots, find old wooden kegs, and cut them in half. The plantings in Hackensack will not be the same as those in Valdosta. This not only helps clean our air, but it can produce much needed food for the underfed in those ghettos. Start first on the inner city schools where the school drop-out rate is frightening, and gangs and pot dealers abound. Those schools are usually flat top buildings. Food is a shortage there, and many youngsters are underfed. Nationwide, hundreds actually die every year from malnutrition.

UrbanAg sends those school dropouts onto that flat roof to grow and sell food to their underfed neighbors. (They have to attend classes to qualify for this money making project.) They can earn money while saving their neighbors and our earth. Unemployed youths can earn money being useful instead of becoming druggies in their idle hours. They might even learn a few things about gardening and marketing. That's better than growing marijuana! Do you think those young gardeners won't plant some marijuana there too? Fat chance! A little supervision is required. Let's have a program to plant tree seeds instead of pot plants—acorns, maple helicopters, pine cones, walnuts, hickory nuts, etc. That's where many of our 50 million saplings will come from for **ArborClean**.

EnerJetts, arise! Here is your opportunity to change the world. Where can you grow saplings? How many? At least, one for every student in your neighborhood schools— probably a few more, so they can have a chance to grow. And then where do you plant the saplings? That is the **EnerJett** challenge. Guide your neighborhood children into productive activities instead of into trouble.

There are many projects that invite local participation. With our disturbing unemployment numbers, small projects don't require large offices or big corporations to get things done locally. Your employer is you neighbor down the street. You can commute to work on foot—no gasoline required! That's what **EnerJett** groups are all about—employing people locally and using local materials. The energy is already there. As they work together on local projects, they will find other local needs that can be tackled by small groups. **EnerJetts** and **DIT** are an answer. They need not be confined to New Energy projects, although that is a prime reason for their formation. The energy problem is immense but lends itself to thousands of small projects as well as a few massive projects. Togetherness works! It's friendly.

Chapter 15

Ocean Currents

Our oceans are in constant motion. Massive amounts of water are moving around Earth and taking energy with them. We have made relatively little effort to capture and use this energy, and it has its limitations. They won't help mid-continent areas much and are not always easily accessible even near our shores. Ocean currents present a challenge to our new technology, but the amount of energy they contain makes it worth our while. Unlike the earlier energy sources we have covered, ocean currents are more suited to a few large installations rather than hundreds of small ones. Here is an opportunity for Big Energy to get a boost from New Energy that is not particularly adaptable to individuals or neighborhoods. They are usually quite remote from neighborhood life, so energy transportation becomes something of a problem. Big Energy excels at that.

Your New Energy is interested in clean energy from any source and wants to use each source where it is most convenient. It favors any clean energy at its most accessible points. Ocean currents are an underused source of energy that comes in large packages. It is most accessible to large industry and can contribute substantially to coastal areas, particularly those with large populations. Many big cities are located on coastlines, because shipping was a prime factor in their population. They can derive clean energy from the very oceans that brought them into existence.

There are two basic kinds of ocean currents. "Gyres" flow in the upper 400 feet of ocean waters, and "ocean currents" flow below 400 feet. There are 6 gyres in the oceans of the world. The North Atlantic Gyre, and the North Pacific Gyre rotate clockwise in circles several thousand miles in circumference. The Southern Pacific Gyre and the Southern Atlantic Gyre rotate counterclockwise. There is also the Indian Ocean Gyre that rotates counterclockwise half of the year and counterclockwise the other half. Finally, there is the Arctic Circumpolar Gyre, which circles Antarctica from west to east. These are currents that can be tapped for energy. The deep water ocean currents carry lots of energy but are relatively inaccessible. These gyres are not usually that close to land, so they have a transportation problem—the kind that Big Energy loves to handle. These massive gyres are slow moving (about 1.5 to 2.5 Mph), but run 24/7/365 days per year. They are huge, so they require large facilities—not the ones for families or **EnerJetts.** Here is Big Energy's boost to offset the loss of domestic energy to local resources. That is another reason to work with instead of against Big Energy.

The Gulf Stream and the Caribbean Loop are portions of the North Atlantic Gyre that come close to land. They have fairly rapid flow and are potential sources of useable energy. Florida Atlantic University is conducting studies of the feasibility of drawing energy from the Gulf Stream. It could supply 1/3 of all of Florida's electric demand, but it also could present a serious hazard to marine life. It continues along most of the east coast and could supply electric power to mid-Atlantic states. There is no use of the Gulf Stream for energy today, but it is of great interest to power companies.

Chapter 16

DIT and Big Energy

Big Energy has opposed the development of local energy sources. They are guilty of the same ossified thinking that they are presenting to the public. They are on the wrong track. Demand for energy is growing. The new demand is primarily in low voltage electronics. Since Big Energy is intimately involved with large AC facilities, they see development of low voltage local supplies as loss of income. But our expanding population increases all energy demands, not just local demands. Industry's demand is expanding as well. Big Energy faces millions of dollars in capital expense to upgrade its outdated AC system. They build huge transformers to replace 300,000 volt high tension wires with 1,000,000 volt wires while the new demand is for 12, 6, and 3 volt sources.

They are trying new and expensive ways to gather enough fossil fuels to satisfy this expanding demand—arctic drilling and Keystone Pipeline. This is a short-sighted view of the future. Instead of entrenching an outdated system of energy, that money and time would be better spent replacing fossil fuels with New Energy. Their profit margins would increase because New Energy is free once the equipment is installed.

Electronics will continue to drive new energy demands. Big Energy is not well equipped to handle that demand. They tend to think bigger, not smaller. Better to allow local energy suppliers to satisfy this new energy demand and focus on finding New Energy sources for their current energy system. Let domestic energy come from domestic sources. Big Energy's market share may be smaller, but their total market will increase. Concentrate on finding new sources for their expanding commercial demand. I am encouraged that they are already using wind in large wind corridors to add to their supply. They build large, expensive wind generators, which take many years to pay for themselves. But their profit margins are greater with the wind than with fossil fuels. And it doesn't pollute!

Scheduled planning could divest the domestic energy demand at the same rate as the industrial demand increases. They could invest in wind, solar, tidal, ocean currents, Tesla free energy or wave technology instead of fracking, arctic oil drilling, and higher voltage transformers. Why do they try to bolster their obsolete system when New Energy sources offer greater profit potentials? I suspect much of that is involved with the profits from coal, gas, and oil that are increasing as the supply gets used up.

I am discouraged by Big Energy's self-congratulatory ads about becoming the world's largest gas and oil suppliers. They are going the wrong way! Instead of the United States becoming the #1 *producer* of fossil fuels, we should become the world's largest consumer of clean New Energy. Here is an opportunity for Big Energy to gain profitability on a growing energy demand. They could advertise that they can reduce your electric costs by moving to clean energy, but they focus on making more money with Old Energy. Indeed, it takes substantial capital to create New Energy sources, but it also takes capital to upgrade their obsolete system. Long term, the odds strongly favor the New Energy sources that can't be used up. Perhaps they could go on a "Green is Clean" campaign and gain public acceptance as well as improved profit margins. "Alternate Energy" is clearly the next big wave in societal development.

Like the railroads of the late 1800s, the automobile of the early 1900s, and the electronics of the late 1900s, New Energy will dominate the next 50 years. It will create hundreds of thousands of jobs, and if we do it right, it will not create any monster corporations to bleed all the profits to the Koch brothers. Since the energy, the materials, and the labor are scattered everywhere there are users, this is an opportunity to create a cottage industry where controls lie locally with the users, not with a few corporate magnates. Here is an opportunity to reverse the recent trend of putting ever more profit and money with ever fewer wealthy people and ever less of it with everyday people. Why do billionaires want to make more money?

Big Energy talks about all the jobs they are creating. Keystone Pipeline jobs will last for perhaps a year or two. New Energy has more jobs to offer than Old Energy. They are long-term jobs as we build and maintain the energy system of the future. What's more, they will be cooperative jobs. Currently, fossil fuel jobs in the Mideast are competitive, not cooperative. American oil money is financing the conflicts in the Mideast. We intervene primarily because of our interest in their oil. Americans don't really understand all the religious conflicts in the Mideast. Our presence there has made us unwelcome and unloved. We are the bad guys the jihadists want to eliminate. We should not get involved with conflicts we don't really understand. Going to New

Energy could eliminate our dependence upon fought over Mideast fossil fuels. Join the wave of the future.

Big Energy need not lay off their oil and coal workers. They should retrain them in New Energy. Those workers would love to learn how to install solar panels, wind mills, and geothermal systems. They might even learn to make and sell Tesla Free Energy systems. Instead of unemployment, we have an opportunity to create millions of jobs worldwide—far more than the jobs we eliminate in coal and oil.

We have witnessed an enormous expansion in social media worldwide. People naturally like to work together. Cooperation is human. Small **EnerJett** groups are a form of social media. The phenomenal expansion of social media tells us that we had a natural craving for togetherness that wasn't being satisfied. New Energy is another source of togetherness that also saves us money and ultimately saves our earth. Get involved! **DIT!**

Chapter 17

Wave energy

Your New Energy focuses primarily on small local sources and actions. But New Energy is everywhere and can benefit large facilities as well. Wind blows over the three quarters of the earth's surface that is water, as well as over the land. Wind is not the sole source of waves but is a major contributor. These waves carry massive amounts of energy that can be utilized. This is not the stuff for local **EnerJett** groups but is yet another way for Big Energy to increase its sources as well as its profit margins. I found five start-up companies trying various techniques for capturing wave energy from our oceans. None has gone commercial yet, but there is much promise there.

Aqucadoura Wave Farm in Portugal was the first. Aquamarine in Scotland was also an early contender as was Oceanlinx in the U.S. The United States Air Force has an operation called Terminator, and Oceanpower Technologies is another American company developing ocean wave power. There is so much power there that there will assuredly be many more companies capitalizing on wave energy. **EnerJetts** should encourage this activity since it gives Big Energy more opportunities to improve their energy resources rather than discouraging small or individual energy sources as they do now.

The basic principle behind wave energy is utilizing large floating drivers that rise and fall as the waves pass them. They are attached to underwater generators that are driven by the oscillating activity of those floating drivers. Since wave height and frequency are measurably different in different areas and at different times, they must be attuned to their location. Although the general technology is the same for all of these devices, the details of operation differ because of their location. The obvious task of the wave energy companies is to make the payback ratio shorter than other New Energy sources in their location. There aren't a lot of other energy sources out in the ocean, so precise location is a critical issue. In addition, wave patterns are not permanently fixed, so careful planning is a part of the process. There must also be some flexibility in the design and operation of the devices to accommodate changes.

I envision another opportunity here. The other prime source of New Energy in our oceans is ocean currents. Although they are not completely independent, ocean currents and ocean waves are basically unrelated. Locating a wave energy system in an ocean current allows the possibility of having the anchored wave system contain waterwheels to capture the ocean currents at the same time. This could double the output of a single device, making the payback period much shorter.

New Energy presents a challenge to the ingenuity of us all. *Your New Energy* has covered many opportunities, but rest assured, there are many more that we haven't even considered. It is my hope and belief that it will stimulate ideas and concepts that will return us to the environment that created us all and will sustain us far into the future.

Chapter 18

Cost or investment?

There are costs for getting into free New Energy. Think in terms of payback period—how long does it take for any savings you create to pay for the equipment you had to install? There is enormous variation in this figure. Some of it depends upon the area in which you live. In bright, sunny states like Louisiana, solar systems can pay for themselves in 4 to 7 years. But beware. New Energy is indeed new, and the expertise for putting it to use is also new. There are huge differences in installation cost, which, almost without exception, will be more than the equipment costs. That is why I strongly favor local **EnerJett** installers right in your neighborhood. Sadly, many professional installers are more interested in making money than in saving you money. Installation costs of solar systems range from about what the solar panels cost to over 5 times their cost. Always get at least three quotes and try to use local entrepreneurs as much as possible. Solar systems can pay for their installation in anywhere from five to twenty-five years. More of that difference comes from installation practices than from your geographical location. I believe that with your local **EnerJett** labor you can get the payback period below 4 years. It is worth the effort.

Apply to your state and federal government—they have substantial subsidies to help you go solar. There are also several independent organizations that contribute to New Energy installations. The Department of Energy (DOE) and National Renewable Energy Laboratory (NREL) are prime places to start. Many banks also have low-interest loan programs for Renewable Energy.

Wholesale prices for solar panels hover around $0.73/watt for massive shipments. The price for individual systems on the open market varies from around $2 to over $5. **EnerJetts** should be able to stay below $2/watt. Remember, when you install a solar system, you are almost invariably installing a battery system as part of it. That expense can be shared if you plan ahead for other New Energy devices that need storage batteries (wind and hydro).

I looked at a system for my 7-bedroom home in Vermont. I found that I could probably install a solar system for about $19,000 (55-month payback). However, the very first quote I got from an outfit that had never even seen my home was $50,000—a payback of over 12 years. I think with local **EnerJett** labor I could install it for about $15,000—a 40-month payback (small local crew, no management expense, no massive equipment moving requirements).

Calculating the savings is something of a trick. I calculate that a properly placed solar panel will generate power about 10 hours per day for 300 days per year. A 120-watt panel will generate 360,000 Watt Hours per year (120x10x300). Current average cost of electricity in the U.S. is 15 cents per KWH (large variations are caused by location and weather conditions). At that price, each panel should generate around $54 of electricity per year, so it is clear that the price of the panel (installed) is critical. Look at your electric bill, and determine how many panels will pay that bill. 10 panels save $550/year; 30 panels save $1650/year. If thirty panels cost you $20,000, they will pay for themselves in 12 years. By Doing It Together with your **EnerJett** neighbors, you might get that cost down to $12,000 and bring the payback to 7 years.

When you calculate how many panels you will need, remember that you will not cut down the wires to your power company. Install just enough panels to cover the average annual usage. In very heavy months, you may still get a small electric bill, but in quiet months, they may pay you. If you install more and require them to pay you monthly, you will hasten the day when the electric company will pass legislation to eliminate their obligation to pay you for extra electricity. Look at it this way. If everyone installs excess New Energy capacity, the electric company will have negative income and go out of business. How will you dry your laundry in December?

Chapter 19

The Upside of Electronics

The marvel of electronics has changed everyday life in America—in the whole world! We use electronics to do what we did ourselves just ten or twenty years ago. We seem content to sit and watch things happen that we strained to do back then. There is a big difference between getting electrons to help us and getting electrons to do it for us. Few of us have replaced those activities with new goals and activities. That is a downside of electronics. It encourages people to let someone else do it. Where is the ambition to do it better or to create something new? That certainly is not for a lack of things that need to be done. We have a serious unemployment problem. We are destroying our environment with our profligate use of outdated fossil fuels. Our schools are not training our youth to cope with the problems facing the future world—illegal immigration, racial discrimination, and political focus on conflict instead of problem solving. We are becoming lazy—and fat! We have brought truth to that old saying "Fat, Dumb, and Happy."

There is an enormous upside to electronics. Since 1985, U.S. industry sent 12 million jobs overseas and gave China the biggest financial boost it has had in three centuries. In 30 years, we have increased our imports from china from $6 million to $38 billion. That left 9 million Americans without jobs while giving China the largest employment they have ever had. China's massive economic gain need not be at the expense of our unemployed. We have removed 9 million

American buyers from our market. Our electronics industry provides employment opportunities for every one of them—directly as well as by educating them on the techniques of future industries. Electronics distribute that information everywhere. Anyone can get it. We need no huge factories or corporate masters.

I am disturbed by the massive collection of ads for retirement. It's as if the objective of life is to retire. But life is about accomplishment—not about munching goodies in front of the television screen. Our wonderful medical system has increased our life expectancy (and our health) about 15 years in the last century. We are wasting those added healthy years. What we need is a change of profession. Set new and different goals. Do things you have dreamed about for the past 25 years. Use electronics to learn about industries that didn't even exist when you were born. We should increase the eligibility age of social security 6 months every year for the next ten years. Create incentives to enjoy productivity instead of inactivity. Is there a problem with being healthy and productive? At least you are not bored.

There is another problem with our current system. Most commercial activities began with a clever product or idea. Those that were helpful or useful grew. As they grew, they began to merge and acquire each other, making ever bigger corporations. The stated reason for those mergers and acquisitions was to increase efficiency. But the real driving force behind those mergers was to gain market control. Without competition, giant corporations can set their own price. They increase their profit margins. The net result is that money goes in ever bigger quantities to ever fewer people. Here is the source of our growing income gap. The rich get richer, and the poor get poorer because the wealthy also have control of wages. "Why should I hire you at $12/hr. when I can hire an Indonesian for $3/hr. or a Kenyan for $1/hr.?" The wealthy buy political control to further entrench themselves. We are building an oligarchy—not just in the U.S., but worldwide. Fewer people have greater control. And now they are fighting among themselves for even greater control. The world has far too many conflicts financed by oil money. New Energy as a cottage industry would minimize or even eliminate that source of conflict.

Enough! It's time for a change. Those huge corporations did not build modern society. They capitalized on it for their own benefit. It's time to return to the "cottage" industries that created today's world. That will require initiative from the man-in-the-street—the initiative that the electronics industry has suppressed. But that same electronics industry also presents enormous opportunity. It brings advanced technology to that very man-in-the-street who is currently unemployed or underemployed. We don't need massive factories to create our daily goods. The raw materials, the labor, and the skills are literally everywhere the user is, and electronics provides the ability to coordinate them into our lives.

Clean New Energy is a prime opportunity. Everyone needs energy. But New Energy's components are in every community. No massive factory is needed. No controlling "Boss" is required to tell you how to do it. **EnerJetts** can get it on the Internet! Small groups in every community can do the job, and the results need not be sent hundreds of miles to the user. Not only will this employ people locally, but it will undermine that control Big Business has on our everyday lives. We should build no more massive industries, and most especially not in foreign countries. We need not build a 2-billion-dollar automobile factory in Mexico to serve our citizens with Mexican labor. We need to put substantial import taxes on American goods imported by this country from low-wage countries.

There are thousands of things needed in our country that cannot be done by anyone outside of the United States. Changing our outdated fossil fuel energy supply to what I call New Energy (solar, wind, tidal, hydro-, geothermal) is a major one. No one in China or Mexico can put a windmill or a solar panel on your roof in Indiana. But your unemployed factory worker neighbor can. We all think New Energy is someone else's job. But it is a fascinating new technology that needs creative new ideas and lots of work—jobs! New Energy will change dramatically in the next decade. Standing the world's largest industry on its head is a massive challenge. That's several million jobs. It will require training—that same training that made this country great. Instead of laying off the coal miner, retrain him in solar or geothermal energy. We increased our productivity by new devices and by training people in productive skills. That is the crux of **DIT**. Increased productivity allowed us to increase wages. Is that what today's schools are teaching our youth today?

41% of U.S. citizens 25 or older have *only* a high school diploma. Another 20% have bachelor's degrees. Our high schools tend to guide people toward college, but college is not for everyone. Who will build the desks and computers they use at work? The world needs both intellectual skills and mechanical skills. Today's 18-year-olds either go to college or take unskilled jobs at low wages. We need much more emphasis on trade schools in today's economy. Seven billion people need trillions of man-made things. Who will build those tools of tomorrow? That's not what colleges teach.

We have been creating larger and larger corporations that employ thousands of people. For the past 25 years they have been building manufacturing plants outside the U.S. to capitalize on low wages there. There go our U.S. Jobs. Ford is building a 2-billion-dollar plant in Mexico. That's 4,000 United States jobs sent to Mexico. Doesn't Ford see that that is 4,000 fewer buyers for automobiles in the U.S.? And we wonder why our economy is struggling? To discourage the outflow of U.S. jobs, we must impose import tariffs on goods manufactured in low-wage countries. If those tariffs are directly related to the wage differences, that will produce progressive wage increases in poor countries, reducing the tariff and reducing the incentive for U.S. companies to build factories elsewhere.

Chapter 20

Nuclear Energy — A Limited Resource

Nuclear energy abounds. But Nuclear Energy is seriously handicapped by its history. It comes from radioactive materials that are hazardous and are dominated by their potential for making nuclear weapons. Most governments monopolize nuclear materials that can produce energy under carefully controlled conditions. In addition, most nuclear energy facilities are huge — not the sort that you can put in your back yard or basement. Since nuclear raw materials are radioactive, they generate an invisible hazard — you need a sign to know that they are there. These are not materials you want lying around your homes or schools.

There are about 550 nuclear power plants in the world. They all produce large amounts of electricity as their energy output. They are not small. They produce from about 500 megawatts to about 4,000 megawatts each. Every one of them is either sponsored by or operated by a government. Safety requirements are daunting. In the United States, they supply about 8% of our electricity. I know of no small nuclear facility designs that would supply a home or even a neighborhood. I see no effort to make small nuclear facilities primarily because of the hazards of the raw materials. It seems unlikely that nuclear power will become a major source of local electricity.

Because of the potential for making nuclear weapons, allowing nuclear materials to flow freely through society is a risk few, if any, nations want to allow. Fortunately, the refining and manufacture of nuclear fuels is a complex and expensive process that does not lend itself to small or clandestine operations. Since there are many other less hazardous and less expensive sources of energy, I do not expect much change in that situation. I do favor the use of existing large nuclear facilities since they are a way of depleting the vast store of weapons grade nuclear materials that are officially designed never to be used. If they were, all life on the planet Earth would cease. Few of us would like to see another Hiroshima or Nagasaki, and today's nuclear weapons are many times as powerful as those weapons.

So far, the International Atomic Energy Commission has maintained fairly close control on these nuclear facilities. Nuclear waste is still a serious problem. Some of those waste products provide nuclear radiation that can be useful elsewhere in society, primarily in medical radiation treatment, but there is a large overabundance of them. I'm not sure we are making effective use of that resource. There seems to be no shortage of radiation for medical treatment. A far bigger problem exists in smaller nations that want to build nuclear weapons. I suspect more of that is for status and political power than for their use as weapons. In fact, most nuclear weapons are designed never to be used. Man and nations still have enormous egos. Since nuclear materials are so powerful, many leaders of small nations want them to gain political power in the world community. That poses a serious hazard to the entire world. I see no simple solution to that problem, and we must keep a worldwide alert to such ego-driven efforts to acquire nuclear weapons. The best approach I see to that problem is to try to minimize international conflicts and encourage cooperative efforts by all nations. Remove the incentive to developing such devastating devices.